Charles Baudelaire

BELGIUM STRIPPED BARE

Translated with an introduction by
Rainer J. Hanshe

Contra Mundum Press   New York · London · Melbourne

Translation *La Belgique déshabillée*
© 2018 Rainer J. Hanshe

Translated from Charles Baudelaire, *Fusées – Mon cœur mis à nu – La Belgique déshabillée suivi d'Amœnitates Belgicæ*, édition d'André Guyaux (Paris: Gallimard 1986).

First Contra Mundum Press
Edition 2019.

All Rights Reserved under
International & Pan-American
Copyright Conventions.
No part of this book may be
reproduced in any form or by
any electronic means, including
information storage and retrieval
systems, without permission in
writing from the publisher,
except by a reviewer who may
quote brief passages in a review.

Library of Congress
Cataloguing-in-Publication Data

Baudelaire, Charles, 1821–1867

[*La Belgique déshabillée*. English.]

Belgium Stripped Bare / Charles
Baudelaire; translated from the
French by Rainer J. Hanshe

—1st Contra Mundum Press
Edition
352 pp., 5 x 8 in.

ISBN 9781940625287

   I. Baudelaire, Charles.
  II. Title.
 III. Hanshe, Rainer J.
 IV. Translator.
  V. Introduction

2019936600

0–lv Introduction: The Spleen of Belgium! *Correspondances, Razzias, & Self-Flagellation*

0–240 *Belgium Stripped Bare*

242 Notes

264 Appendix: Shakespeare Tercentenary Letter to *Figaro*

THE SPLEEN OF BELGIUM!
Correspondances, Razzias, & Self-Flagellation

In early 1864, as Baudelaire continued to suffer difficulties with publishing his writing, he was in severe financial straits and plagued by ill health, including recurrent outbreaks of syphilis, cardiac arrests, and violent attacks of neuralgia. Two years prior, even though they were already optioned by Poulet-Malassis, his principal publisher, Baudelaire sold the rights to the publication of several of his works, including a second edition of *Les fleurs du Mal*, in order to ward off his pursuing creditors but, like the ventures of many gamblers, the poet's wager did not end favorably. If intoxication is a number, this exceedingly negative one is not, and what Baudelaire called his *guignon*, the evil spirit of misfortune and disaster, continued to plague him. Shortly thereafter, on November 12, 1862, Poulet-Malassis was arrested and incarcerated in the Clichy debtors' prison for owing his printer, Poupart-Davyl, 14,000 francs,[1] then transferred to the more severe Madelonnettes Prison, where De Sade and Chamfort were confined during the French Revolution.

1. One of Baudelaire's close friends, photographer Félix Nadar, was also incarcerated in the same debtors' prison and wrote an anonymous article (signed F.-T. Molin) about his internment titled "Clichy in 1850." One thrust of Nadar's essay is how some debtors are driven mad by the conditions and that the prison only demoralizes and dishonors its inhabitants. See *Le National* (February 8–23, 1851) and *Le Voleur* (March 25, 1851).

When Poulet-Malassis was declared bankrupt, it necessitated the sale of his entire catalogue, which included several of Baudelaire's works,[2] thereby effectively silencing the poet's voice through his no longer being in print. After serving five months in jail, Poulet-Malassis was condemned by the court, a judgment he would seek to appeal.[3] Control of Baudelaire's inheritance still remained in the hands of Narcisse-Désiré Ancelle, his family lawyer, too, with Baudelaire receiving only 200 francs a month on which to live (the equivalent of around $40); if he needed additional funds, it entailed a humiliating series of entreaties and genuflections, but they often yielded nothing. With this desultory situation before him, in late 1861, the poet bid for a seat in the prestigious Académie Française. Knowing very well that it was an aristocratic bourgeois institution that would surely not elect a poet of his ill repute, if Baudelaire's pursuit of the candidacy were a provocation, it was also equally genuine. The writer felt that he deserved the seat, and as a gambler, what was there to risk, save for suffering possible humiliation? There was something in him that relished wounds, or wanted to test whether his *guignon* would continue, or the spell finally be broken. The chance of possibly striking pay dirt compels the gambler to bet the devil his head, even if the odds of winning are improbable.

---

2. *Les fleurs du Mal* and *Les Paradis artificiels*, both of which were remaindered at 1 franc ($0.19) a copy.

3. Little is known of this trial and judgment since the judicial records were burned during the Paris Commune in 1871.

If awarded the candidacy, it would result in Baudelaire being deemed one of the prestigious 40 'immortals' of the Académie Française and his gaining financial security once and for all. With the condemnation of *Les fleurs du Mal* shadowing him, and his general reputation as an immoralist and provocateur, both Lamartine and de Vigny (themselves immortals) warned him that the results would most probably be demoralizing. When de Vigny urged him to retract his appeal, Baudelaire mentioned that, on Saint-Beuve's advice, he had already officially declared his candidature. Eventually, in early 1862, following an ambivalent article by Saint-Beuve, who, if saluting Baudelaire, cast him as a figure of the margins and purveyor of the bizarre, stupefied on hashish, opium, and other drugs, the poet acquiesced after de Vigny finally dissuaded him against further pursuing his appeal. That grand escape route from debt thereby evaporated in Baudelaire's hands.[4] He had repeated bouts of vertigo as well, noting in *My Heart Laid Bare* that he "suffered a strange warning" after one such incident: "I felt the *wind of the wing of imbecility* pass over me."[5] Some months after that abyssal premonition, on April 14, 1862, Claude-Alphonse Baudelaire, the poet's half-brother, died from the effects of a cerebral hemorrhage compounded by a hemiplegic stroke. Although he had not seen him for twenty years, his half-brother's demise seemingly provoked

---

4. For more details, see Claude Pichois, *Baudelaire* (1989) 291–99.

5. *My Heart Laid Bare*, tr. by Rainer J. Hanshe (2017) §86.

in the poet the fear of his own possible early death. Gambles not yielding fortune, the body in the midst of disintegration, the word vanishing into oblivion, the horizon for Baudelaire was growing ever more tenebrous. Spleen, *oui*; ideal, *non*.

When Poulet-Malassis' bid for a pardon was rejected in late April of 1863, he was ordered to serve one more month in Madelonnettes Prison. Once out of jail, he suggested to Baudelaire that they head to Belgium, that less censorious and more liberal country, where they could perhaps flourish, and Baudelaire would be free to pursue his artistic endeavors without condemnation or retaliation. Despite his own reputation as an immoralist, Baudelaire's taste was contrary to that of his publisher; nonetheless, he decided to join him in Belgium and planned to give lectures on art, write for the review *L'Indépendance belge*, and try to gain favor with Lacroix and Verboeckhoven, the publishers of Victor Hugo, in hope that they would publish *Les Paradis artificiels* and at least two volumes of critical essays (*Curiosités esthétiques* and *Opinions littéraires*). Since Hugo and Baudelaire were acquaintances, Baudelaire asked the esteemed writer to intercede on his behalf, making him certain that the results would be positive, and his fortune would finally change.

In mid-September, Poulet-Malassis would depart Paris & take up residence in Ixelles. Two months later, Baudelaire surrendered in perpetuity the entirety of the greatest source of his income, his prized translations of his doppelganger Edgar Allan Poe, to yet another publisher, Michel Lévy. Expecting something in the vicinity of 30,000 francs for his translations, instead, Baudelaire was offered the paltry sum of 2,000 francs (around $375) for a decade plus of work.[6] Yet, even that pittance would never reach the poet's hands but immediately go to those of his creditors. One cannot help but think here of that satiric but pained self-portrait of Baudelaire's wherein he depicted himself before a winged sack of money — fortune, he seemed to predict, would remain perpetually beyond his grasp, like fruit before the hands of Tantalus. Such were the dark & desperate circumstances surrounding Baudelaire's journey to Belgium.

On April 24, 1864, Baudelaire departed for Brussels with something of a massive shipwreck in his wake. Rather quickly, the darkness would only intensify, if not grow truly nefarious, and the wreckage become ever more terrible, then ultimately fatal. All of Baudelaire's envisaged projects would come to nil, and his spiral into spiritual vertigo would begin. "I came to find peace," he later told a friend, "a chance to work, to escape the pressures of Paris life. [...]

---

6. Consider two contrasting examples to see how slighted Baudelaire was: 1) Victor Hugo received 120,000 francs from his Belgian publisher for two books, *Les Chansons des rues et des bois* and *Les Travailleurs de la mer*; and 2) Jules Janin received $2,000 a year from the *Journal des Débats* for his weekly report, $1,200 from *Indépendance belge* for his column, and $1,500–$2,000 from new editions of his old works, or from new publications or contributions to magazines. His total income was reported as being between $6,000–$8,000 per year. The figures (in dollars) about Janin are taken from the *American Literary Gazette and Publishers' Circular*, Vol. 5 (1865), 70.

Besides, I am sick, sick."[7] And in a letter to painter Édouard Manet, Baudelaire tells his friend that the "Belgians are fools, liars, and thieves. I've been the victim of the most shameless swindle. Here deceit is the rule and brings no dishonor." He explains further that he is "considered to be an associate of the French police by people here. Don't ever believe what people say about the good nature of the Belgians. Ruse, defiance, false affability, crudeness, treachery — now all that you *can* believe."[8] Outcast in Paris, pariah in Brussels. The poet's *guignon* did not relent.

Are those statements, as a number of Baudelaire's letters from that period and his notes for his projected Belgian book, the paranoid ravings of someone in the final throes of syphilitic madness, as they are often characterized? Are they the cynical, dyspeptic ranting of a sickly misanthrope, a person whose mind has been ravaged by decades of indulging in opium, wine, and hashish, as Saint-Beuve believed? Or is there some validity and truth to Baudelaire's observations? Are they in fact the keen, lucid, measured perceptions of a clear thinking and sober-minded *flâneur*?

1864 was the year of the tercentenary of Shakespeare's birth and jubilees were to be held for it in numerous cities around the world. In an article in *Le Moniteur Universel*, Théophile Gautier outlined the Parisian jubilee & everything

---

7. Alex De Jonge, *Baudelaire: Prince of Clouds* (1976) 209.

8. May 27, 1864 letter. See *Selected Letters of Charles Baudelaire: The Conquest of Solitude*, tr. & ed. by Rosemary Lloyd (1986) 203.

it would entail, which included a procession along the grand boulevards of Paris, performances, and a celebratory banquet culminating with the publication of Victor Hugo's new book *William Shakespeare*. A French Shakespeare Committee was being formed and Hugo was to be elected its Honorary President, as engineered by his family & coterie of acolytes. Still an exile and archenemy of Louis-Napoléon,[9] the occasion was an opportunity for the political refugee to enter the Parisian if not world stage again, albeit as a royal specter. Part of the Parisian jubilee included Hugo being represented by an empty throne draped in black fabric and beheld as a kind of omnipotent king (the idea was that of Hugo's wife). Considering his political disposition, the gesture was not perceived as a mere literary coronation: Hugo was being touted as a leader no less than the current emperor, and so, far more than just the self-elected inheritor of Shakespeare's mantle. Since the event was to occur at the Grand Hôtel, a building personally supervised by Louis-Napoléon, the entire affair led to an uproar within the emperor's circle, which perceived

9. Hugo had been in exile since December 11, 1851 when, along with a host of other radicals considered a danger to the French nation, he was expelled by Louis-Napoléon "from French territory, from Algeria, and from the colonies, for reasons of general security..." *Constitutionel* (January 11, 1852). Quoted in William VanderWolk's *Victor Hugo in Exile* (2006) 67. Recall that Devil's Island was opened in 1852 and some of its first prisoners included nearly 250 republicans who opposed Napoléon's *coup d'état*. Hugo, if not possibly Baudelaire, could very well have ended up there.

it as a symbolic attack on the government. One could also see the empty, funereally draped throne as an invocation of the emperor's assassination, or at least of his being deposed. In *Napoléon le petit*, Hugo did depict the emperor as a criminal for violating the constitution and thus someone who should be dethroned.

What pray tell does all that have to do with Baudelaire? Ten days before leaving for Belgium, the *poète maudit* wrote an anonymous letter of nearly 2000 words to *Figaro*'s editor-in-chief, condemning the entire spectacle, subtly explicating the self-serving politicization of Shakespeare's legacy. Hugo is one of the primary targets of Baudelaire's article and he first underscores the subversive nature of the jubilee by referring to Hugo's participation in the 1848 revolution and the alliance made between his literary school and democracy, an alliance Baudelaire characterizes as adulterous, monstrous, and bizarre. Thereafter, the attacker says, "Olympio" (a sarcastic nickname for Hugo) renounced the doctrine of art for art's sake to take up the doctrine of art as revolutionary propaganda. The jubilee is then described as nothing more than a blatant publicity stunt meant to "incite the success of V. Hugo's book on Shakespeare" which, "like all of V. Hugo's books, is full of beauties *&* stupidities," and that it "may once again vex his most sincere admirers […]."[10] Considering that Hugo

---

10. "Anniversaire de la naissance de Shakespeare," *Œuvres complètes de Charles Baudelaire*, Vol. XI, ed. by Jacques Crépet (1939) 217–222. Tr. by RJH. All further quotes of the *Figaro* letter hail from this source.

and Baudelaire were, if not close friends, certainly frequent correspondents and sometimes acquaintances, Baudelaire's gesture was peculiar, if not strangely self-destructive. There is also considerable irony in his decision to raise the matter with *Figaro* since two articles they published condemning certain poems of his most probably led to the trial of *Les fleurs du Mal*.[11] Perhaps he figured, if *Figaro*'s articles led to his condemnation, then Hugo too would be condemned *&* he would usurp the royal specter.

Aside from Olympio, one of Baudelaire's other targets was Jules Favre, an opposition deputy and lawyer who was being appointed to the Shakespeare Committee despite his not being a man of letters. It was Favre's appointment that seemed to most incense Baudelaire, if not be a direct insult, since the poet refers to himself in the third person in his letter, stating that "M. Charles Baudelaire, whose taste for Saxon literature is well known, had been forgotten." Clearly outraged, the poet, essayist, and translator of English literature sarcastically notes that Favre is "sufficiently cultivated to understand the beauties of Shakespeare, *&*, as such, he can attend; but if he has two *liards* of common sense, and if he wishes not to compromise the old poet, he has only to refuse the absurd honor conferred on him. Jules Favre in a Shakespearean committee! This is more grotesque than a Dufaure at the Academy!" Baudelaire ultimately castigates the whole

---

11. See Pichois, *op. cit.*, 223–24.

event as "a great stupidity" and "monstrous hypocrisy" and urges it be denounced.

The letter was explosive, with repercussions sounding not only in France, but elsewhere, including England, whose own proceedings in honor of the Bard were eclipsed by Hugo's plot. It was less Gautier's informative article and more Baudelaire's incisive interpretation of it that ignited the backlash. Since Leon-Napoléon's regime considered Hugo and his cohorts to be subversives, as Marie-Clémence Régnier notes, "Baudelaire's letter set off an alarm among members of the government. The *'conseil des ministres'* consequently decided to ban the French and English banquets at the Grand Hôtel."[12] To the emperor's cabinet, the event was seen as an illicit political assembly. While the ban had financial consequences for Hugo's faction, if not himself, it also had governmental repercussions. Diplomatic relations between the French and the English were disturbed by the ban since the English Ambassador had consented to participate in the Parisian event. *The New York Times* reported that "Nothing that the Emperor has done for a long time has made him more unpopular with the English Parisians, and it seems unaccountable that he should have taken this step just after Lord Clarendon's visit, and the announced restoration of the *entente cordiale*."[13] Since the Republican opposition petitioned

---

12. Marie-Clémence Régnier, "Shakespeare's 1864 Jubilee in France," *Shakespeare Jubilees: 1769–2014*, ed. by Christa Johnson & Dieter Mehl, 120.

13. "The Shakespeare Tercentenary," *The New York Times* (May 8, 1864) 2.

to overturn the ban, which "contradicted Louis-Napoléon's will to liberalize his politics and to maintain peaceful relations with the Republication opposition,"[14] it lent their cause ever-greater legitimacy, with support coming from England and elsewhere, including Stratford-upon-Avon, where the French flag was set at half-mast.

A seemingly innocuous Shakespeare jubilee became an event of international intrigue, took on a cast of revolt, and reinforced the fact that Hugo, who a few years earlier had refused the general amnesty (for the second time) issued by the Second Empire, was a continuing threat to the French state. Whilst organized opposition to Napoléon III intensified, Belgium was pressured to extradite any fomenters. As Graham Robb notes, "Belgian Parliament responded by tightening controls on foreigners." During this episode, "Hugo was accused by the Belgian Foreign Minister of 'corrupting the young,'" "copies of *Les Misérables* were burned publicly in Spain &, in June 1864, Pope Pius IX anticipated the choice of posterity by adding *Les Misérables*, *Madame Bovary*, and all the novels of Stendhal and Balzac to the Index Prohibitorum."[15] Baudelaire's role in instigating the skirmish is apparent enough, even if the international repercussions that unfolded from it were far from his intention, nor willed by him. One week after penning his destructive screed,

---

14. Regnier, *op. cit.*, 120.

15. Graham Robb, *Victor Hugo: A Biography*, 401–02.

he wrote to the painter Arthur Stevens, telling his friend, a Belgian, that he wanted to see the publisher Lacroix, "to whom *perhaps* (!) Victor Hugo wrote a word for me."[16] That *perhaps* and parenthetical exclamation could not be more darkly pregnant. While Hugo did supposedly write to his publisher on behalf of the poet in December of the preceding year, knowing even then that Baudelaire was virtually his enemy, with the advent of the Shakespeare affair, Hugo, if not his cohorts, imaginably brought the potential relation between Baudelaire and Lacroix to a halt. If outrage can lead to a book being a *succès de scandale*, it isn't always the case. Less an analysis of Shakespeare and his plays and more a pamphlet for Hugo's political pronouncements, the book was a critical failure and roundly ridiculed in France, with Hugo being deemed a self-aggrandizing lunatic. His publishers must have been furious with Baudelaire. As Poulet-Malassis later wrote, Lacroix "never on any account wanted to meet Baudelaire, and always behaved toward him in the most stupidly vulgar fashion. Baudelaire detested him, and had every reason to do so."[17] As sympathetic to Baudelaire as one might be, it is easy to understand why his actions incurred contempt.

The rumors that Baudelaire was a spy reporting on Republican exiles in Brussels on behalf of the French police occurred swiftly after the Shakespeare fiasco, & Baudelaire

16. Baudelaire, *Œuvres complètes*, II (1975) 356.
17. September 8, 1867 letter. See Pichois, *op. cit.*, 322.

had no doubt that it was "the Hugo gang" that spread them. Baudelaire's sudden appearance in Brussels immediately following the fracas probably only made the rumor more believable. In a letter to his mother, he says that "that infamous noise comes from Paris, it was launched by someone from the V. Hugo gang, very familiar with Belgian stupidity and credulity. It is revenge for a letter I published in Paris, where I mocked the famous Shakespearean banquet."[18] In *The Writer of Modern Life*, Walter Benjamin suggests that Baudelaire's reputation in Belgium could "hardly have been only his manifest hostility toward Hugo" and that Baudelaire's "devastating irony contributed to the origin of that rumor."[19] To Benjamin, Baudelaire "may have taken pleasure in spreading [the rumor] himself," but in light of the aforementioned facts, that is doubtful. If out of his fury with the Belgians Baudelaire did spread other mordant rumors about himself (that he was a murderer, a pederast, a Jesuit, etc.), they were made after his denunciation as a spy. As should be evident, the matter is undoubtedly far more labyrinthine than Benjamin makes out, especially considering the fractious personal circumstances, and such fraught political undercurrents. It is hardly surprising then that, when Baudelaire gave the first of his lectures in Belgium, Hugo's publishers were absentee.

18. June 11, 1864 letter. L.B. & F.E. Hyslop, *Baudelaire: A Self-Portrait* (1957) 203–05.

19. *The Writer of Modern Life* (2006) 49.

While Baudelaire's first lecture, "Eugène Delacroix, the Painter and the Man," was highly esteemed, his second, on Gautier, was hapless, for he began by making a double entendre about losing his virginity as a speaker and it scandalized the attendees, mostly Belgian women, teachers, and schoolgirls, all of whom swiftly scurried out of the lecture hall. A number of people remained, including a very young Claude Lemmonier, who spoke of the lecture in effusive and grandiloquent terms, noting how Baudelaire's voice "swelled and rang like the voice of a preacher" & that his "patrician hands" "traced slow evocative patterns through the air" and "accompanied the musical cadences of his sentences with halting, hovering gestures that were like mystic rites."[20] However captivating his ritualistic performance may have been, Baudelaire undermined himself with his black humor. As Lemmonier reports, the audience further dwindled, and the lecture ended with a door rapidly banging and the usher removing the lamp and exiting: "I remained in the darkness where the voice of that father of the literary church had died away."[21] With even fewer attendees, the third lecture was more disastrous, Baudelaire trembling nervously, not engaging with the audience, staring downward at his papers. The fourth was cancelled. If Baudelaire's aim of trying to impress Lacroix and gain him as a publisher was already doomed, the aftereffect

---

20. W.T. Bandy & Claude Pichois, *Baudelaire devant ses contemporains* (1957) 211.

21. Ibid.

of his lectures certainly solidified the matter. With his ill-fated standing as a lecturer, his plan to tour other cities fell through. The darkness and silence in which Baudelaire's second lecture ended seemed to presage the darkness & silence in which his whole Belgium period would end.

Presumably ignorant of the devastating effect of his *Figaro* salvo, & that it made him *persona non grata*, Baudelaire attempted to attract Hugo's publishers yet again by staging a party at which he would offer wine, food, and recitations of his poetry. Of the 30 invited people, only ten came, and of that small number, two left not long after the proceedings began. Lacroix and Verbœckhoven did not attend, and so Baudelaire's hopes of finding refuge in print in Belgium were sundered. Other publishers treated him with equal disdain or ill regard. Imaginably with a heart full of bitterness and a great sense of doom, Baudelaire began outlining his future book on Belgium, originally intended as a series of letters he sought to publish in *Figaro*. The range of provisional titles suggests the variegated approaches he had in mind: *Poor Belgium! Grotesque Belgium, The Capital of Apes*, and *Belgium Stripped Bare*. The multitude of headings throughout his notes indicates the expansive scope of his vision, with observations ranging from those of a sociologist to an anthropologist, city planner, æsthete, and more. Through Baudelaire's fleeting eye, we witness sketches of his examination of physiognomy (of humans, streets, and architecture), political customs, the fear of annexation by France, general traits or characteristics, including observations about animals, women, love & prostitution, cuisine, health, and related questions of tobacco & wine, economy, familial matters, social relations and hospitality, crime and punishment, bigotry, the French language in Belgium, everyday phrases, *bon mots*, journalism and literature, style, religion, burial customs, oddities and amusements, the fine arts, modern painting and museums, churches, landscapes, streets, and walking or, to Baudelaire, the art of the *flâneur*. A veritable full-scale examination of every aspect of life, viewed from a host of guises, Baudelaire's perspectival eye catching a world in a glance.

In perusing this material though, it is imperative to keep in mind that it is not in fact a finished book but rather a plethora of notes and vast collection of related newspaper clippings (not included herein, but summarized in brief under each related heading) that Baudelaire was to refer to for further analysis and development of his project.[22] When reviewing Baudelaire's manuscripts after his paralysis, Poulet-Malassis said of *Pauvre Belgique!* that "it is nothing but a jumble of notes — not one line written."[23] It is risky to make definitive judgments of such a non-work, as Derrida and other critics have done. Nonetheless, we have a clear enough indication of what it might have been and can read the material with greater perspicacity.

---

22. The newspaper and other clippings Baudelaire preserved illustrate that his analyses of every aspect of Belgium were not limited to his own perceptions and observations.

23. *Les derniers mois de Charles Baudelaire ... correspondances*, documents, ed. Jean Richer et Marcel A. Ruff (1976) 19.

What kind of book was *Pauvre Belgique!* to be? Baudelaire began the work in 1864, a period during which Lavater's belief that each individual's character was imprinted physiognomically (almost like a trademark, or what the French call a *poncif*) and served as a sort of hieroglyph open to scientific interpretation still prevailed.[24] Lavater's influence was not limited to the visual arts, but had an equal impact upon literary forms of representation, too. While Baudelaire found certain aspects of his approach ill conceived, he thought his guiding principle sound, and *Pauvre Belgique!* is, in part, a kind of physiognomic work.[25] In the very first section of Baudelaire's notes, he states outright that he will be making "a sketch of Belgium" and that, as a satire, the work has the double advantage of being "a caricature of the follies of France." Immediately, the nature of the proposed book is clear — it is not single, but double. If Belgium is its focus, that poorly assembled faux country (Baudelaire refers to it as a diplomatic harlequin) is but an effigy that will serve as a simulacrum or corresponding mirror of France, an aim that is born out even in the existing fragments. In other notes

24. That same year, Cesare Lombroso published his physiognomic study of genius, *Genio e follia* (*Genius & Madness*). In one of his later works, Baudelaire figures as a case subject and is deemed "the type of lunatic possessed by the *Délire des grandeurs*." See *Man of Genius* (1896) 70.

25. Baudelaire refers to Lavater in numerous works, including his "Choice of Consoling Maxims on Love," "The Salon of 1846," "The Universal Exhibition of 1855," and "Some French Caricaturists."

(§4, §206, §339), Baudelaire makes parallels between Belgium and America, thereby extending his simulacrum across the Atlantic, further multiplying it, making the proposed work a kind of repeating carnival mirror. *Pauvre Belgique!* is also a sketch, thus a quick impression, yet not a work of realism, a genre Baudelaire detested, but caricature. As with his beloved Daumier, caricature for Baudelaire is a moral act, and as described in his essay on laughter, its highest form is *le comique absolu*, which he relates to the 18th C. genre of the grotesque. Such caricature involves a sublime form of laughter, or mad, excessive hilarity one could refer to as Democritean, for it exults over mankind's follies. And in his letters, Baudelaire further explains that the book is "expressed in highly comic terms" and that it "is a very grave, very severe sketch, severe in its suggestions, under a frivolous, at times excessively frivolous, guise."[26] Despite such precise characterizations, great misunderstanding remains about how to interpret the work, which is largely taken at face value. Interpretations more in line with its true character are in order.

In his analysis of Marcel Broodthaers' blank edition of Baudelaire's *Pauvre Belgique!*, Craig Douglas Dworkin characterizes Baudelaire's text as "mean-spirited" and a "condescending cultural critique," entirely blind to Baudelaire's black humor *&* the satirical nature of the *intended* book. Dworkin claims that Baudelaire sees "his subject as an essay *'du rien*

---

26. *Selected Letters, op. cit.*, 243.

[on nothing],'" and that "the book is characterized (or caricatured) by absence," referring to Baudelaire's observations of there being no sidewalks, no gutters, no toilets, no stalls, etc., and that even Baudelaire's description of the abundance of balconies is negative: "there is no one on them."[27] This entirely inaccurate account is a manipulation of one phrase wherein Baudelaire begins to outline the merits of "making a book on Belgium," part of which includes the desire "to be entertaining when speaking of boredom" and "instructive *when* speaking of nothing…" (§2, emphasis added). It is not an essay solely *on* nothing, and the aforementioned observations are quite factual, what an urban planner of the time might observe about the city. Master plans to rebuild Belgium had been conceived by King Léopold as early as 1861, & in 1865, the city architect of Brussels, Leon Suys, was in the midst of preparing a redevelopment plan for the city. Soon after Baudelaire left, Brussels would in fact be partially quarantined. One wonders if Dworkin even read the entirety of the notes since they are not solely comprised of reflections on absence, nor caricatured by such either.[28] One passage alone suffices to undermine his

---

27. *No Medium* (2013) 176.

28. In the very same passage, Baudelaire enumerates his further intentions — after the aim of being "instructive when speaking of nothing," he continues: "to build on the point of a needle; to dance on a loose rope; to swim in an asphaltite lake, or in dormant water" (§2). Alternatively, in §10, he writes: "Make an entertaining work on a thankless subject." Hence, the notes present contrasting views that belie Dworkin's definitive judgments.

claim of absence or negativity being the guiding compass of the book: "Flowers in very great quantities. Rooms with a moderately wealthy appearance. In the back, an overstuffed little garden. Amazing resemblance between all apartments. Seen from up close, the luxury is not only monotonous, but trashy" (§33). As established, Baudelaire's critique of Belgium is manifold, and covers everything from physiognomy to law, literature, religion, politics, justice, & more.

In *Given Time*, the most damning judgment of all is made against Baudelaire when Derrida speaks of the poet's "anti-Belgian xenophobia, indeed racism," something he says we dare not find humorous.[29] The philosopher next refers to a "genocidal passage" from the poet's confessional *Mon cœur mis à nu* to substantiate this viewpoint: "Fine conspiracy to organize for the extermination of the Jewish Race. The Jews, *Librarians*, and witnesses of *Redemption*."[30] In his psycho-biographical study of Baudelaire, Sartre similarly charged the poet (he may have been the first to do so) when claiming that Baudelaire himself "declared that he was anti-Semitic."[31]

---

29. In judging Baudelaire on this, European critics (especially French) should consider their own generally accepted antipathy to the United States. As Jesper Gulddal has noted, "Chauvinism toward the United States is an integral part of European culture, which can be traced back to the second half of the 18th C., and it has manifested itself continuously (albeit with varying degrees of intensity) right up until the present day." See Jesper Gulddal, *Anti-Americanism in European Literature* (2011) 2.

30. MHLB §82, p. 151.

31. Jean-Paul Sartre, *Baudelaire* (1950) 67.

If numerous scholars repeat this charge, seemingly aping Sartre and Derrida, Walter Benjamin dismisses the passage on extermination as a peculiarly French form of humor, *une gauloisserie*, as does Claude Pichois, the editor of Baudelaire's complete works, who states that the passage is not very easy to interpret and therefore "any [charge of] anti-Semitism is to be dismissed."[32] If Derrida is justified in rejecting such counter claims and correct that the charge of anti-Semitism not be too easily cast aside, Pichois' view that the passage is difficult to interpret demands more consideration than Derrida is willing to give it, for we cannot definitively ascertain that the statement is Baudelaire's personal viewpoint. It could very well be one he overheard in the streets of Belgium, especially since his notebooks do contain many pronouncements made by others, most of which are not set in quotemarks.[33] James Lawler urges that "we need to keep the ironies implicit in the text and context well in mind," and also suggests that "'fine conspiracy' is, or would appear to be, black humor directed as much at himself as at any other. Above all, in Judas, and the Jew of the two stanzas [...] in 'Les Sept Vieillards,' the poet discovers his own portrait: the Jew is less the Other than himself."[34] And since Sartre gives no reference for his

32. Quoted in Derrida, *Given Time* (1992) 130.

33. Since Baudelaire did not complete either MHLB or BSB during his lifetime, and some passages could be included in either book, the true home of the quote remains radically in question. Is it Baudelaire's heart laid bare, or Belgium's?

34. James Lawler, *Poetry & Moral Dialectic: Baudelaire's "Secret Architecture"* (1997) 202, footnote 12.

claim, nor quotes any passage wherein Baudelaire makes such a declaration, his assertion lacks credibility. It could have ballast if it were substantiated with further analysis, or the citation of other passages in Baudelaire's work or letters that reveal some trace of anti-Semitism, but those two lines seem to be the sole fragments of their kind in Baudelaire's *œuvre*.[35] Contrarily, there is a passage in *Pauvre Belgique!* under a section titled "Brussels / Customs" wherein Baudelaire writes: "General crookedness. Beware the Jews! Beware especially the German Russians! What is the German-Russian. Some fine examples of Belgian crookedness" (§116). Based upon the section title, & the final phrase, is Baudelaire not in fact speaking of the prejudices of the Belgians, and could not the 'genocidal' passage be part of *their* crookedness, not the poet's?[36]

35. For an extended analysis of Baudelaire's supposed anti-Semitism, see Brett Bowles, "Poetic Practice and Historical Paradigm: Charles Baudelaire's Anti-Semitism," PMLA, Vol. 115, No. 2 (March 2000) 195–208. Bowles' final conclusion is that there is no valid basis for seeing Baudelaire as a disseminator of anti-Semitism or precursor of anti-Semitic French reactionary thought. He does however believe that, psychologically, "Baudelaire's case illustrates the historical transition between traditional and modern anti-Semitism" (207). The article is full of wild readings, historically inaccurate translations, the manipulation of completely disparate texts, and other instances of faulty logic. Considering Bowles' own conclusion, even the subtitle of his article is misleading.

36. Derrida does not cite this passage, nor does Sartre, nor any other commentator. Of note too is the fact that Baudelaire's first great love, Sara, was Jewish.

In the very next section, he discusses their hatred of strangers and notes that no one is more inclined to rejoice in the misfortune of others than the Belgian. "*Universal* barbarism and vulgarity, without exception, with the lively affectation of civilized manners. *Manners* !!!" To Baudelaire, such schismatic characteristics are evidence of only more hypocrisy.

Recounting several invectives of Baudelaire's against democracy, progress, and human rights, Derrida vociferously asks his reader who would accept such exclamations, who would accept sentences "that ought to wring cries of protest today from all the champions of liberal democracy"?[37] Although Derrida's humanist denunciation is seemingly righteous, democracy and progress are not inherently positive, nor free from critique. To Baudelaire, progress is not born of the hive, of the masses, of people "who can think only in common, in herds," but it arises "through the individual and by the individual alone."[38] It is not therefore that Baudelaire opposes progress *en générale* (it has multiple valences for him), but that it cannot be measured at the level of the species. In one apocalyptic vision of the world in *My Heart Laid Bare*, the principal focus of Baudelaire's attack is mechanization (an abuse and mishandling of technology one could see in Heideggerian terms) and progress (as

37. Derrida, *op. cit.*, 130–31.
38. MHLB §83.

catastrophe and ruin)[39] and their evisceration of our spiritual character. Consider America, that great bastion of democracy, at the time of his diatribes, for that nation is the focus of his critique: blacks were considered ⅗th of a person, slavery was legal, the Native American population had suffered genocide while not one treaty made to them had been honored, women did not have the right to vote, and many of America's writers, such as Poe (one could think of Melville & others), endured moral opprobrium or, to invoke Artaud, were eventually suicided by society. It is largely through Poe and his life and reception that Baudelaire sees America, for it is the relationship between the writer and society that becomes the measure of the country's values and spirit. After studying Poe's life, Baudelaire is persuaded that "the United States was for Poe a vast cage, a large accounting establishment, and that all his life he made sinister efforts to escape the influence of that antipathic atmosphere."[40] Baudelaire lambasts American critics, who become representative of democracy itself, for

---

39. For example, the absentminded 'modernization' of cities, which often includes the destruction of historical architecture and the elimination of poor districts, not only the erasure of the past then, but often the further marginalization of the poor through deliberately engineered gentrification. Specifically pertinent here is the decimation of the medieval and Renaissance fabric of Brussels, most of which was destroyed during its 'modernization.'

40. Baudelaire, "Edgar Allan Poe. Sa vie et ses ouvrages," Œuvres posthumes (1908 ; 3e éd.) 189–241. Translated by RJH. For an existing English translation of Baudelaire's material on Poe, see L.B. & F.E. Hyslop, *Baudelaire on Poe: Critical Papers* (2014).

suggesting that Poe normalize his genius by using his creative faculties in ways more appropriate to American soil, that is: not to disturb the peace, not to write arcane works of superior intelligence, but to write family books and to be "*a money-making author.*"[41] What true democracy is there, intimates Baudelaire, if a writer of Poe's genius is forced to prostitute his art in order to live? If he is forced, that is, to suppress his individuality in favor of a social being entirely alien to his character? To Baudelaire, the powers that Poe had to wrestle against betrayed nothing less than the spirit of tyranny:

> Democracy has its disadvantages, that, notwithstanding its benevolent mask of freedom, it doesn't always allow the expansion of individualities, that it is often very difficult to think and write in a country where there are twenty or thirty millions of sovereigns, that, moreover, *you have heard* that there exists in the United States a tyranny much more cruel and inexorable than that of a monarch, which is that of public opinion … [42]

---

41. Ibid. To Borges, the tradition of admiring Poe against the United States was perfidious, a wave started by Baudelaire and extended by Shaw. "Poe," Borges says, "would have suffered in any country." That is contentious, and Baudelaire suggests that Poe would have found friends in Paris or Germany who would have understood or relieved him. See Herman Diaz, *Borges: Between History and Eternity* (2012) 85–86.

42. Baudelaire, "Edgar Allan Poe…" *op. cit.*

In a different tenor, nearly three decades earlier, De Tocqueville had written of a similar threat after his visit to America. Although he expressed admiration for certain aspects of American society, De Tocqueville warned that there was a pernicious side to equality: in the atomization of the individual, society becomes of the greatest importance, and that results in every citizen "being assimilated to all the rest"; the individual is then "lost in the crowd, and nothing stands conspicuous but the great and imposing image of the people at large."[43] The interests and privileges of society usurp those of the individual, whose interests and privileges are effaced, or of no value to the behemoth that is Nation. It is then that "the power which represents the community has far more information and wisdom than any of the members of that community; and that it is the duty, as well as the right, of that power to guide as well as govern each private citizen."[44] And so the society of the panopticon is born. For De Tocqueville, such leads to the "tyranny of the majority" or, in Baudelaire's words, the patriot "would gladly pass over the solitary and free souls, and trample them under the feet with as much insouciance as his immense railroads, cut down forests, and his monster-boats, the remains of a boat burnt the day before. He is so anxious to arrive. Time and money, everything is there."[45] Derrida is clearly thinking of some ideal, purist

---

43. Alexis de Tocqueville, *Democracy in America* (2002) 607.

44. Ibid.

45. Baudelaire, "Edgar Allan Poe..." *op. cit.*

notion of *Democracy* when judging Baudelaire's critique, for the philosopher could surely not defend such a base and corroded form of politics. The poet excoriates the hypocrisy seething beneath the spectral façade of freedom, knowing full well the pernicious outcome. Such democrats are too good, Baudelaire says, "not to hate their great men, and the ill will that pursues Poe after the lamentable conclusion of his sad existence recalls the British hatred that persecuted Byron."[46] The status of the poet is the litmus test of a country's politics, a barometer of freedom.

Baudelaire's critiques of Belgium, France, and America are best thought of in relation to his championing of the individual over society and his critique of democracy and the neutralizing forces of a nation. "Nations," Baudelaire said, "have great men only despite themselves. Hence, the great man is the conqueror of his entire nation."[47] Poe and Byron, two "great men" for Baudelaire, can be thought of as types, figures that represent an absolute form of singularity. They are solitary, free souls, true representatives of the self-reliant, emancipated individual. And is there any figure more marginalized than the *poète maudit*? In not identifying with country, race, religion, nor sexuality, he does not have the ready-made securities that come with identity politics, for he knows that the self cannot be reduced to, nor restricted to, such limited

46. Ibid.
47. MHLB §82.

forms of identity. He has no identifiable costume, no community, no flag. He is large, he contains multitudes. If a democracy is not strong enough to endure an anomaly such as Poe (or Nerval), is it even a democracy? Baudelaire once mused, "Perhaps the future belongs to the *déclassés?*"[48] No. One can imagine Poe, Byron, Artaud, Bene, and others shout in chorus with Baudelaire: "Shall we say that the world has become uninhabitable to me?" (§8) Over a century later, another writer, the Romanian exile Ghérasim Luca, felt similarly, & his last words before leaping into the Seine were: "There is no place in this world for poets."

Derrida, Dworkin, and other critics have lambasted Baudelaire for his supposed prejudices yet, if the tone of the Belgium book is at times trenchant, there is an acute perceptiveness in Baudelaire's observations, many of which prove to be accurate, if not oddly prescient. Although the Belgian poet Georges Rodenbach found the material on Belgium painful, noting that the country is judged severely, he agreed that many of Baudelaire's criticisms were painfully true and that the Belgians knew that better than anyone else.[49] We must remember too that, as Baudelaire made clear, he intended the book to be incendiary ("Livre fait à la Diable" §4), while it is also perhaps an enactment of a desire he expressed in *My Heart Laid Bare* to create a *poncif*, a kind of characteristic

---

48. March 5, 1852 letter. *Selected Letters,* op. cit., 45.

49. See Georges Rodenbach, "Reportage posthume," *Le Progrès* (July 14, 1887) 3.

eikon, for to do so Baudelaire says is an act of genius.[50] Although not a great champion of liberal democracy, consider that Baudelaire is at once making a critique of Belgium, his own country (and thus himself), and America. When writing of *Pauvre Belgique!* in a letter, Baudelaire said "it is time to tell the truth about *Belgium*, and about *America*, the other Eldorado of the French rabble."[51] "France," he observes in one of his notes, "is, undoubtedly, a very barbarous country. Belgium also." Subsequently, he makes the brief but damning conclusion that "civilization may have taken refuge in some small as of yet undiscovered tribe" (§5). If Derrida is to give considerable heft to a single ambiguous passage and use it to condemn Baudelaire, equal heft can be given to Baudelaire's truculent criticism of Europe and the Americas and serve as a counterbalance. It is not in Europe or America that civilization has taken refuge, Baudelaire declares, *but in some tribal community*. What Hegel calls the spirit of history has in Baudelaire's eyes fled the West. The future of humanity lies elsewhere.

If we are to accurately assess the Belgian book, or read it with more discernment, we must also keep in mind what

50. MHLB §20, p. 45. Generally (mis)translated into English as cliché or stereotype (think of its mid-19th C. meaning), *poncif* is a kind of defining feature or artist's trademark. Baudelaire uses it as an æsthetic term referring to gestures and dispositions (affect if you like). In French, it denotes a structural pattern. See §10 of Baudelaire's *Salon* of 1846 for his elucidation of *chic* and *poncif*.

51. February 18, 1866 letter. *Selected Letters*, op. cit., 248.

Alex De Jonge refers to as Baudelaire's shock tactics, his humorous form of provocation, what the French call *pince-sans-rire* (pinching without laughing). In public, the poet frequently made outrageous statements in order to provoke shock, once noting that it is sweet "to be hated by fools,"[52] and the flagrantly evil (the late 14th C. meaning of outrageous) figures throughout his work as well. For Baudelaire, there is no beauty without shock. As he pronounced, "irregularity, that is, the unexpected, surprise, astonishment, are an essential & characteristic part of beauty."[53] Since beauty for Baudelaire is found in the grotesque, in ugliness, in decay, in what others deem morally corrupt, it could be argued that his view of the Belgians as largely 'monstrous' contains a paradoxical form of respect, for they serve as a valid 'subject' for his art. Beauty for Baudelaire isn't classical. He isn't a poet of Raphael's Madonnas, or of ancient Greek sculpture. While Keats and others wrote of Grecian urns, Baudelaire wrote of prostitutes, criminals, rag pickers, exiled gypsies, dogs. If horrified by the Belgians, his continued gazing at them involves some form of scopophilia. To Gretchen Schultz, the book is not an expression of chauvinistic nationalism but instead an elaborate metaphor for hell on earth. Countering Pichois' view of the book as a failure, Schultz argues that it is in fact a supernumerary triumph of erotic delight and "should be read as an *ars poetica* in the negative, as a compendium of æsthetic

52. De Jonge, *op. cit.*, 51.
53. MHLB §32.

and ideological judgments in which 'Belgian' is an arbitrary signifier of the abject ..."[54] And it is not the natural world that is the *topos* of the abject and modernity, but the city. Baudelaire speaks in one letter of being assailed at twilight by daydreams and that, "in the heart of the woods, enclosed beneath those vaults that seem like sacristies *&* cathedrals, I think of our astonishing cities, and the prodigious music that rolls across the treetops sounds to me like the translation of human grief."[55] While in the woods, that quintessential *topos* of the Romantics and all nature poets, a site that Baudelaire says *seems* religious, he thinks instead of astonishing cities and human grief. For that *flâneur*, it is the city which is the sacristy and the cathedral; it is the city which is sacred and spiritual. His is not the equipoise of classicism, but the disorder of evil, of the urban grotesque as beauty. Baudelaire is Satan's litanist, he who praises dogs, the precursor of Artaud, Bataille, and Bene, that legion of the damned.[56]

---

54. Gretchen Schultz, *Sapphic Fathers* (2014) 35, 37. Schultz's interpretation and analysis of the Belgium book is exceptionally discerning and insightful.

55. Letter to Fernand Desnoyers, late 1853. *Correspondance* II (1973) 386.

56. To give one example, focusing on the genealogy between Baudelaire and Bataille, with its images of violent and schismatic subjectivity, sadism, destruction, and monstrous sexual fantasies (the narrator fantasizes about wounding his lover's belly and then penetrating that wound and pumping his blood/venom into it), Baudelaire's poem "A celle qui est trop gaie" (one of the banned poems of *Les fleurs du Mal*) evokes a form of accursed eroticism that prefigures Bataille's entire erotic vision,

Let us now turn to some of the general observations Baudelaire makes about Brussels and the Belgians and, in contrast to myopic contemporary perspectives of them, consider them in more accurate historical light.

In Baudelaire's *catalogus rerum* of Brussels, the general overruling condition is one of blandness and dissolution: record is given not only of the blandness of cigars, but of the blandness of vegetables, flowers, and fruit. All the food is steamed or boiled, made with rancid butter, or doused with salt. The bread, ever fundamental to the French table, is execrable (it is either damp, soggy, or burnt). The cuisine is disgusting and elementary. The eyes, hair, and gazes of people are equally bland, their physiognomy heavy and puffy, most women have eyelids like onion-skin, colorless & empty eyes, retracted jaws, flat feet, elephantine legs, and lilac complexions. "In short, it is the same race as in earlier times," Baudelaire concludes, giving as evidence the figures depicted in early Belgian paintings: "we shall again find in the present life the ankylosed styles of the primitive painters of the North" (§ 38). Although animals have sad & sleepy demeanors, dogs (called the Negroes of Belgium) alone are alive — in them, "the vitality absent elsewhere seems to have taken refuge" (§ 23).

↵ but that is prefigured by Sade. Even Baudelaire's fascination with an image of a Chinese soldier excising the bleeding heart of a victim and eating it calls to mind Bataille's obsession with a horrific lingchi photo as described in *Tears of Eros* (1989) 204–6, *passim*. For the story about Baudelaire and the image of the Chinese soldier, see De Jonge, 51–52.

In one peculiar and disconcerting passage, Baudelaire speaks of a man who becomes prosperous by eating live dogs at town fairs before an audience of women and children. An attempt to gain much needed life? When analyzing the physiognomy of the street, he recounts the Belgian's mania (the word is his) for cleanliness, of how they scrub the sidewalks with black soap even when it rains, and that many people have vitreous eyes. Testing his sight upon the natural world, the now bucolic-*flâneur* remarks upon the woods being sparsely populated and devoid of insects *&* songbirds: "Life scarce in the woods and meadows. The animal itself avoids those cursed regions. — No insects, no songbirds" (§292). The same depopulation is noticeable in the city: "No life in the Street. […] Everyone at home. Doors closed" (§29) When recounting that Brussels is a city of Hunchbacks and the domain of Rickets, questioning why, Baudelaire wonders whether it is due to the water, the beer, or the insalubrity of the city and its housing (§38). The danger of possible infection reaches a fever pitch: "Horrible fear, on the part of the Frenchman, of this *Soporific Contagion*" (§382). Is all this anti-Belgian xenophobia as Derrida charges? Are these the caustic generalizations of an intolerant French nationalist, or descriptions that have some foundation in reality?

In the mid to late 19th C., due to the shift from an agricultural to an industrial society in Belgium, the population exploded, expanding 35% in Brussels alone in an extremely brief period of time. Coupled with the generally wretched condition of the city, significant social *&* health issues arose.

Since the 1850s, the Senne (the river in Brussels that Baudelaire frequently assaults) had become a serious health hazard. Due to the anoxic decomposition of sewage and garbage, the stench of urban rivers such as the Thames in London was so unbearable that "the British Parliament recessed during the affected periods."[57] In Brussels, the lack of proper sanitation contributed to nearly 3,500 deaths due to a cholera epidemic in May 1866, just two months after Baudelaire's aphasic collapse in nearby Namur. The water quality in general in the mid-19th and early-20th centuries deteriorated to such an extent that it led to the construction of flushing tunnels and other sanitary measures. However, as noted in the *Historical Dictionary of Brussels*, "Pollution remained a major issue that was not addressed vigorously until the completion of modern wastewater treatment plants in the first decade of the 21st century."[58] The year Baudelaire died, the entire course of the Senne was completely covered over due to pollution from industrial refuse & untreated sewage, yet, if he didn't establish a precise corollary between his observations and the general contagion that beset the city, even scientists had little concept of disease in the mid-19th C. It was only between 1860 & 1864 that Pasteur had conducted his experiments on the relationship between germ and disease. Nonetheless, the sagacious eye of the poet possessed scientific insight at times.

---

57. Zhao-Yin Wang, Joseph H.W. Lee, Charles S. Melching, *River Dynamics and Integrated River Management* (2015) 556.

58. Paul F. State, *Historical Dictionary of Brussels* (2015) 388.

During a walk from Brussels to Namur, the *flâneur* observes that many shrubs, as the landscape, are blackish; elsewhere, he speaks of the surrounding countryside being filthy and yellowish. Such sickly vegetation could be Baudelaire's exceptionally keen analysis of potato leaf blotch, which is caused by a parasite that forms small, scattered brown spots on leaves. Eventually, such spots spread and form well-defined blackish patches.[59] In his own æsthetic manner then, Baudelaire clearly recognized the different diseases that had infected the country. While frustrated that the innumerable hills made *flânerie* all but impossible, he notes with greater stupefaction that faro, the national drink, "is taken from the great latrine, the Senne; it's a drink extracted from the excrement of the city & subjected to a filtering device. Thus, for centuries, the city drinks its urine" (§50). Consider the effect of that upon the agriculture and physiology of the Belgians. Approaching the matter diagnostically, albeit still æsthetically, Baudelaire wonders whether the general ugliness of the people is related to their inability to appreciate beauty. An obvious satirical comment, since his analyses can also be extremely precise & detailed, such as when he makes a gynecological observation when speaking of women and "the dirty tone of white

---

59. The first severe outbreak of this was recorded in an agricultural gazette in 1845. It was reputed to be so extreme that entire fields in Belgium were desolated. Two years of famine (1845 and 1860) resulting from a similar outbreak in Ireland led to the death of 1 million people and double that emigrating. See David Moore, *Slayers, Servants, and Sex: An Exposé of Kingdom Fungi* (2001) 22, 25, *passim*.

leucorrhea" (§40). So much for Nadar's proposition that Baudelaire was a virgin.

Nearly two decades after Baudelaire left Brussels, the contagion was all too real. Routine inspections of factories were "mandated by the 1885 Manufactory Act, while in Belgium they stemmed from the creation of a ministry for work and industry in 1895. The inspectors' reports for the Montreal and Brussels areas confirm the dangerous and unhealthy conditions denounced by labourers. Year after year, these firsthand witnesses of industrialization condemned the excessive smoke, noise, and dust to which workers were exposed, the lack of adequate ventilation, and the absence of appropriate sanitary installations."[60] As Susan Peterson states, "International health diplomacy began in 1851, when European states gathered for the first International Sanitary Conference to discuss cooperation on cholera, plague, & yellow fever. […] [D]isease control became a subject of diplomatic discussion as a result of the cholera epidemics that swept through Europe in the first half of the 19th century."[61] Baudelaire's observations about Belgium and its people turn out not to be the hyperbolic responses of an oversensitive neurotic poet venting his spleen, but acute perceptions in which he discerned

60. Nicolas Kenny, *The Feel of the City: Experiences of Urban Transformation* (2014) 99.

61. "Epidemic Disease and National Security," *Security Studies*, Vol. 12 (2002) 43–81.

genuine and serious health threats and their impact upon the atmosphere, the body, the cuisine, and more. Much of *Pauvre Belgique!* takes on a sharply different cast in light of the general noxious conditions of the city. The self-declared Epimenides was a genuine seer.

Aside from such factual and diagnostic observations, and the book's comic and satiric nature, it can be seen as a work of the most complex *correspondance*. As Benjamin describes them, *correspondances* for Baudelaire are "the data of remembrance — not historical data, but data of prehistory," experiences that seek to establish themselves "in crisis-proof form."[62] In such light, the Brussels period can be seen as a form of extreme experimentation, a radical encounter wherein, even if not at the conscious level, Baudelaire explored the perhaps most immense *correspondance* of all. It is not a metaphysical, Swedenborgian *correspondance*, but a strictly mortal one — the *correspondance* of his life itself. As noted earlier, Brussels is a double or simulacrum of Paris for the poet and *Pauvre Belgique!* is an oblique attack on a country that never sufficiently recognized Baudelaire's literary genius during his lifetime. "This book on Belgium is [...] a try-out of my claws. I will make use of it later against France. I will patiently express all the reasons for my disgust with the human race …"[63]

---

62. Walter Benjamin, *Illuminations* (1968) 182.

63. Letter to Ancelle, November 13, 1864. OC II, 421.

While the contemned one did have his admirers, by and large his work was not received with the kind of understanding and respect he knew it warranted. His major work, *Les fleurs du Mal*, suffered condemnation and censorship, many of his works were out of print or published only in obscure, largely unknown magazines, and publishing was for him increasingly difficult, a difficulty which, even if partly due to his own actions, doubled itself in Belgium. As an exile, Baudelaire's contempt for Paris finds *correspondance* in its paltry double, Brussels, a bourgeois caricature of the city of lights, with the Seine of Paris finding its double in the Senne of its city, and through the data of pre-history (that of his own and others), the *flâneur* attempts to fathom the dense hieroglyphs not only of Brussels and Belgium, but of Paris and France, and thereby of his life, of Poe's life and America,[64] and ultimately of the place of the poet in society. We could say that he even finds a *correspondance* or double of himself in Belgium in Félicien Rops' father-in-law: "a unique man, a severe and jovial magistrate, a great quoter and a great hunter. The only man in Belgium who knows Latin and looks like a Frenchman" (§295). If the multiplying figure that is Baudelaire — numbers, numbers, number is intoxication! — could be successful in Brussels, then he would at last shatter his ill status in Paris and France, stand triumphant, and simul-

---

64. Baudelaire finds a *correspondance* even between the condemners and acolytes of American and French assassins: "The people who treat Booth like a scoundrel are the same who adore Corday" (§339).

taneously vindicate himself, and thereby Poe as his double for the injustices that they both suffered from their respective countries. For he who enters into the circular continuum of time, that infinite locale where the personal *subjectum* evaporates, every identity becomes an adoptable persona or mask. As Benjamin points out, *correspondances* can "constitute the court of judgment before which the art object is found to be a faithful reproduction, which makes it entirely aporetic."[65] The aporia Baudelaire establishes for himself with this book could not be more intractable, for there are also *correspondances* that offer no consolation, *correspondances* that are ineffectual, and the intoxication of diagnosis miscarries. "The ideal supplies the power of remembrance; Spleen musters the multitude of the seconds against it."[66] If the inevitable miscarriage is apparent, the *poète maudit* soldiers on, for, as every scientist knows, failure doesn't negate the value of an experiment. In depicting Brussels and its free thinkers, artists, politicians, and citizens as apes and hypocrites in general,[67] the poet-writer figure is the implicit counter-figure of truth, honesty, and authenticity. He is the magistrate who examines, appraises, and diagnoses an epidemic. He deciphers the riddle of the plague that besets the city. Œdipus before the

---

65. *The Writer of Modern Life, op. cit.*, 287.

66. Benjamin, *Illuminations, op. cit.*, 183.

67. The wives of the freethinkers not being permitted to go to mass or confession, drunken Redemptorists preaching against drunkenness, irreligious priests, etc.

Sphinx. He is the great man as the conqueror of an entire nation. It is Baudelaire as the conqueror of Belgium/France, and as the third subterranean *correspondance*, he is or *becomes* Poe and the conqueror of America. When speaking of electoral politics in Belgium, Baudelaire notes how "the stupidity of this people resembles the stupidity of every nation" (§ 237), thereby extending that possible *correspondance* to the entire world. Baudelaire's victory is not a question of financial success, nor is it even one of artistic achievement. It is a victory in regards to the act of analysis itself, of the intoxication of diagnosis, of a superior moral *&* intellectual acuity. Even though the book is unfinished, not a book, it remains a triumph. In Belgium, there is no Latin or Greek, no philosophy, French is spoken poorly, there is a hatred of poetry and all literature, a hatred of beauty and wit, and great art is ignored in favor of *municipal* painting. Even the military is a kind of faux entity according to Baudelaire, for it engages in nothing but rhetorical exercises: "Reports of imaginary battles. Sad comfort in inaction" (§ 244). Belgium is in fact so abject that it takes on the most accursed metaphysical status of all — it is the *correspondance* for Baudelaire of the Inferno itself:

> It has sometimes occurred to my mind that Belgium was perhaps one of the graduated hells, scattered throughout creation, and that the Belgians were, as Kircher believes of certain animals, ancient criminal spirits and abject beings enclosed in deformed bodies. (§ 312)

The passage is clearly satiric, evidence of Baudelaire's satanic humor: he sets in motion the enactment of a punishing *telos* of repetition — the only explanation for a *species* such as the Belgians is that they are ancient criminal spirits reborn in deformed bodies. What is our punishment if we ourselves transgress? "We become Belgian for having sinned." For the Belgian, it is a case of double down: "A Belgian is his own hell" (§312). To take that at face value, Derrida has to be seriously lacking in a sense of humor. Baudelaire's mordant wit has escaped him; black irony evaporates in his fingers. All the same, if we extend the logic of the *poète maudit*'s proposal, within his satiric construction that is, Belgium (and so, in this hall of reflecting *correspondances*, France & America?) becomes the equivalent of Evil. What to do with such a pestilential entity, or how to save the culture within it from contagion? It must of course be seized. "Notice to any European Army," Baudelaire commands. "*Never annexation. But still the Razzia. We have to start with that*" (§318). Intriguingly, despite his call to a European army for this imagined attack, Baudelaire uses the word *razzia*, French for the Algerian-Arabic *ghazw* (غزو), which the OED defines as "a hostile incursion, foray or raid, for purpose of conquest, plunder, capture of slaves, etc., as practiced by the Mohammedan peoples in Africa."[68]

---

68. Regardless of the more accurate meaning of the term within Islamic studies, Baudelaire understood the word *razzia* to denote a specific type of raid, as did most others of his epoch, and that is how he uses it. For further explanations of the term, see Ludwig W. Adamec, *The A to Z of Islam* (2009) 110, and A. Al-Dawoody, *The Islamic Law of War: Justifications and Regulations* (2011) 22, 23.

INTRODUCTION

Only a European army enacting an Afro-Islamic form of incursion will safeguard us from Belgium and preserve the cultural heritage of the world. Europe + Afro-Islam — that is the saving hybrid formula; that is the redemptive equation. So much then for Baudelaire's supposed xenophobic and colonialist tendencies. Belgium, France, and America is the axis of evil that must be defeated. Satanic wit here reaches its apex. The fomenter continues: "The *razzia* of monuments, paintings, art objects of all kinds. The *razzia* of riches. You can transport everything that is beautiful. Every nation has the right to say: *It belongs to me, since the Belgians do not enjoy it*" (§318). Belgium is the tyrannical stupid Nation and every other nation is the avenging Poet conquering the tyrant. It is the preservation of greatness that is at stake. It is a metaphysical question of Good vs. Evil.

Implicit in Baudelaire's observations are numerous questions: How is Belgium (and its doubles) a democracy? How is it a nation? If a poet of Baudelaire's ilk can suffer the indignities he did in Paris and Belgium (and Poe in America), how is either a culture? *En plus.* "To the critic, to the unwelcome observer," notes Baudelaire, "Belgium, somnolent and brutalized, would gladly reply: 'I am happy; do not wake me up!'" (§308) It is such apathy, it is such mollusk-like vegetative (non)-being that the poetic magistrate is in combat with. If victorious, the *poète maudit*'s victory is the victory of the all-seeing *flâneur*. He becomes the quintessential icon of dignity and nobility while exposing bogus communal values, for he has the highest ideals in mind. In a mere fleeting glance, he projects before us in his reflecting mirror a portrait of a dissolute nation, of a false democracy, of bogus notions of progress, of bankrupt human rights, of a polis which, in favor of monetary gain, demands conformity (and so the erasure of the individual) and allows corruption, pollution, and disease to predominate and poison its character. "Belgium is a *shit-covered stick*; that is above all what constitutes its inviolability. *Don't touch Belgium!*" (§ 239) The country has degenerated to such a degree as to have become hell and, in that, it is the taboo *par excellence*. "*Noli me tangere!*" (§ 306) Baudelaire declaims, uttering to the contaminated the warning of one who has returned from the dead, a return that signals no less than a coming apocalypse. Belgium is however only a simulacrum of an inferno, its river a counterfeit one of that most infamous of rivers. Nonetheless, its imminent fall is in sight. Here is Baudelaire's final vision of that graduated hell:

> Today, Monday, August 28, 1865, on a hot and humid evening, I wandered through the labyrinth of a street fair, a *Kermesse*, and in the streets named *Devil's Corner*, *Monks' Rampart*, *Our Lady of Sleep*, *Six Poker Chips*, and several others, with great delight I happened upon, suspended in the air, an abundance of signs of cholera. Have I invoked it sufficiently, that beloved monster? Have I studied well enough the advance signs of its arrival? How long is it, that horrible beloved of mine, that impartial Attila, that divine scourge whose victims are haphazard? Have I

sufficiently begged the Lord My God to quicken its flight over the stinking banks of the *Senne?* And how I will delight in observing the death-throe grimaces of that hideous people entangled in the coils of its counterfeit-Styx, its *Briarious river*, which contains even more excrement than the sky above nourishes flies! — I shall delight, said I, in the terrors and tortures inflicted on that yellow-haired, naked, & lilac-colored race. (End sheet #7)

This too is a *razzia*, for the warring poet says elsewhere that he "would not object to an invasion and a *Razzia*, in the ancient manner, in the manner of Attila. Everything beautiful can be brought to the *Louvre*. All this belongs to us far more legitimately than to Belgium, since they no longer understand it" (§352–61, #21). Baudelaire's prophetic end of the world vision of America ends similarly, with its downfall coming about because of dissolution as well as due to an abasement of the heart. What is refined will degenerate and "nothing will remain of the entrails but viscera! — That age," the reluctant prophet concludes, "is perhaps very near; who knows if it has not already come, and if the coarsening of our nature is not the sole obstacle that prevents us from evaluating the environment in which we breathe!"[69]

---

69. MHLB §22. This excoriating vision of America has come true and its myriad facets are unfolding like wildfire and have been for some time.

In such a diagnosis, we see that to become insensate is one of our great dangers, for that impedes our ability to accurately assess our existence and transform it.

The same month of that enraged vision and call for a *razzia*, Baudelaire devised the alternate title *Une capitale ridicule* for his Belgium book. The caricature finds its fitting mask; the *eikon* has been forged. Later that year, in December, Baudelaire refers to it as *La Belgique déshabillée* — the veil has been torn away; the flesh has been revealed. But this insight into the *correspondance* will soon come to an end. Further violent attacks of neuralgia ensue, then, in the New Year, more such attacks, dizzy spells, and nausea. While Mallarmé, Verlaine, and other new young poets celebrate Baudelaire's work in Paris, the all-seeing *flâneur* visits Namur on the invitation of Rops and his father-in-law. The effect of the various sites upon him is extraordinary. As Rilke turned from the eye to the heart, Baudelaire turned from the spleen to the eye. The impression of Boileau and Van der Meulen, he says, remained in him the entire time of his stay. He is so overwhelmed by the sight of three churches there (the Récollets, Saint-Aubin, and Saint-Loup) that he remarks to himself that he must characterize the beauty of their style (late Gothic). "A particular art, composite art. In search of origins (De Brosses)." And in his speaking of the solemnity of the 18th C., one thinks of his comments on beauty and how melancholy is one of its necessary components. Obviously, he found nothing melancholic in Brussels. "Keep working," he spurs himself on, clearly stimulated by his journey.

INTRODUCTION

The church of Saint-Loup is a sinister and gallant marvel to him and differs he says from everything he has seen of the Jesuits. "Confessional, all of a varied style: fine, subtle, baroque, a *new antiquity*. The *Beguinage* church in Brussels is a communicant. *Saint-Loup* is a terrible and delicious catafalque. The general majesty of all those Jesuitical churches, flooded with light, with large windows, boudoirs of Religion..." De Sade writes *La philosophie dans le boudoir*, Baudelaire thinks of *boudoirs of Religion*. The phrase, the idea, is astonishing. He is so impressed with Saint-Loup that he commands himself to record the experience: "Technical description (*as much as possible*) of Saint-Loup" (§303, emphasis mine). In Antwerp, he is surprised to find an admixture of the novel and the ancient: "New (!) and ancient fortifications with English gardens." The parenthetical exclamation is once again pregnant, but this time with an almost ecstatic joy, for it precedes something remarkable, the discovery of a genuine city: "Finally, here is a city that has the air of a great capital" (§295). The eye has awakened him, he is transformed, his spirit is alight. He seems to be inspired to write yet another book, too, in opposition to Victor Hugo: "Philosophy of the history of architecture, *according to me*" (§352–61, #25). His body however would not persist, and those descriptions and philosophies would never come to be. Baudelaire collapses, suffers a cerebral stroke, and is left hemiplegic and mute.

Speculation abounds regarding both why Baudelaire remained in Brussels when he detested the city so intensely, and why he could not complete what in the end he came to call *La Belgique déshabillée*. To Nadar, the poet's extended stay from a projected mere few weeks to just over two years "could be explained in his tormented life by a vague need to escape himself."[70] François Meltzer believes that Baudelaire's reasons for staying so long in Belgium are not entirely clear, yet while she acknowledges the poet's need to escape creditors, she agrees that Nadar's guess is as good as any.[71] To Pichois, Baudelaire's continued presence in Belgium was surely another sign of his maniacal obsession with loathing the Belgians & expressing his disgust for them. "If Brussels was so revolting, why not return to Paris? His reasons for staying on were specious."[72] Pichois, who is typically acute in his interpretations of Baudelaire, seems in this case to be as mistaken as Nadar & other critics. The principal concrete reason why Baudelaire remained in Belgium was undoubtedly due to debt. Pichois and others are blind to the very real threat of the poet being imprisoned, which was a constant and quite disturbing possibility to him.

As noted, since both Poulet-Malassis and Nadar had been jailed for debts, Baudelaire had intimate accounts of the debtors' prisons and the severe conditions he would suffer were he ever to be arrested. If a complaint was lodged against him by any of his creditors, and he had many, returning to

70. Nadar, *Charles Baudelaire: Intime* (1994) 117. Cited in Meltzer.

71. Françoise Meltzer, *Seeing Double: Baudelaire's Modernity* (2011) 61–62.

72. Pichois, *Baudelaire, op. cit.*, 322.

Paris could have led to his eventual arrest. Considering he didn't have the constitution — let alone wealth — of the Marquis de Sade, it is doubtful he would have survived incarceration. It is far from the dandy's preferred milieu and, in fact, Baudelaire had first-hand knowledge of confinement since, when younger and healthier, he spent several days in Hôtel des Haricots, the prison of the National Garde de Paris, for failing to do his compulsory service in the late 1840s. Clearly, he did not want to risk his freedom ever again and preferred being on the run. In Brussels, his stay at the Grand Miroir incurred enough debt to compel his concierge to visit him whenever he received a letter in case it contained any money. After continuous disturbances, the writer redirected his correspondence *poste restante* simply not to be pestered on a regular basis. But she was the only creditor he ever encountered in Brussels and his debt to the Grand Miroir was insignificant enough not to warrant his imprisonment. In a June 9, 1864 letter, Poulet-Malassis notes that Baudelaire is "so amazed at this city in which, with the exception of myself, he never meets a single creditor."[73] The absurdity of his entrapment resulting from his debts is evident when he writes to Ancelle on October 13, 1864, stating that he "has to go back to France in order to get some money, & I need some money in order to leave, — and also to go on another excursion to Namur, Bruges, and Anvers (to do with art and architecture;

---

73. June 9, 1864 letter. Pichois, *Baudelaire, op. cit.*, 326.

six days at the most). So the whole thing's *a vicious circle*."[74] In another letter to Ancelle, Baudelaire explains why an intended trip to Paris never occurred, recounting that he was so incredibly affrighted, he could not risk the journey. He compares himself to a terrified animal:

> At the last moment, the moment of leaving, [...] a feeling of terror seized me, *the terror felt by a frightened dog*, the horror of seeing my hell once more, of passing through Paris without any certainty of being able to make payments large enough to assure me real peace of mind in Honfleur. And so I wrote letters to newspapers and to friends in Paris and to the person to whom I've entrusted the business of selling my four volumes, the very ones I had come to offer so credulously to Lacroix.[75]

And his fear of possible imprisonment is ever more palpable when, on New Year's Day of 1865, he writes to his mother and says that he is "terrified of being in Paris with no money, of staying in Paris — my hell — for just six or seven days, without giving a few of my creditors some definite assurances. I do not wish to return to France until I can do so covered in *glory*."[76] Brussels is hell. Paris is hell. There is no escape.

---

74. Ibid., 322.

75. Hyslop, *Baudelaire: A Self-Portrait, op. cit.*, 211.

76. Ibid., 213.

L

INTRODUCTION

The inferno is everywhere, the circumference nowhere. Such is spiritual vertigo for the damned. Recall too that, in each of Baudelaire's notebooks, he obsessively enumerated his every debt and expense, tallying them up in precise detail as if he were an accountant, intermingling them with his writing plans as if one determined the other. The fear of debt reaches such an apex of terror that a Poe-like anecdote about a debtor suffering nothing less than cannibalism by his creditors is recorded in *La Belgique déshabillée*. The Frenchman here is clearly Baudelaire:

> If one learns that a Frenchman has money, one keeps him preciously, to eat him. Then, when he is ruined, he is thrown abruptly into prison for Debts, where new phenomena of exploitation take place (the bed, the table, the chairs, etc.). Thus Belgian hospitality (which applies to all travelers) is political economy, or cannibalism. (§ 337)

In *My Heart Laid Bare*, Baudelaire defines glory as being the payment of debts (§ 92). Is it not irrefutable then that the poet was pinioned in Brussels due to crippling poverty? What is particularly unjust about his financial situation is that, when he died, a total of 30,500 francs remained of the inheritance he received from his father, but the restrictive hand of Ancelle forever kept Baudelaire from managing it himself. If the dandy was profligate in his youth, he may not have been so in his later years — he did not have to suffer the iniquities of poverty to the extreme degree that he did.

As for Nadar's hypothesis, Baudelaire was surely not naïve enough to believe he could escape himself in Brussels. To the wife of his friend Paul Meurice, Baudelaire explained that, "whether I'm in Paris, Brussels, or a strange town, I can rest assured that I'll be sick and incurable. There is a form of misanthropy that comes, not from having a bad character, but from being too sensitive & too easily shocked. Why do I stay in Brussels when I hate it? *First of all, because I'm there*, and because in my present state I'd be uncomfortable wherever I was; secondly because I'm doing penance."[77] Beyond the lacerating guilt he experienced over his debts, & the paralyzing fright at very likely being imprisoned for them, I believe he also remained in Brussels due to the sheer intractability of struggling to confront and surmount what I interpret as a *correspondance* of such immeasurable scale, of an aporia so impassable, at least in his poor health, and with his *guignon*. The *poète maudit* did not seek to escape himself as Nadar proposes, but to remain in Brussels so as to burrow ever deeper and deeper into himself, to enact a repeated ritual of self-flagellation. It is a question of penitence. Such necessitated his remaining in 'hell.'

"Les bons chiens" was the last work published while the *poète maudit* who felt the terror of a frightened dog was still alive, and like the calamitous dog of that *poème en prose*, he too sought to create some form of *bonheur* out of his misery:

---

77. February 3, 1865 letter.

I praise the despicable dog, the poor dog, the homeless dog, the flâneur dog, the saltimbanque dog, the dog whose instinct, like that of the poor, the gypsy, and the stage actor, is wonderfully sharpened by necessity, that very good mother, that true patroness of intellects!

I praise the calamitous dogs, those who wander, lonely, in the sinuous ditches of great cities, or those who with their blinking and spiritual eyes have said to forsaken men: "Take me with you, and with our two miseries, perhaps we shall create a kind of happiness!"[78]

---

78. "Les bon chiens," *Œuvres complètes de Charles Baudelaire*, IV. *Petits Poèmes en prose, Les Paradis artificiels* (1869) 146–150. Tr. by RJH.

A NOTE ON THE TEXT

Letters or words crossed out by Baudelaire have been set between square brackets [ ]; letters or words added by him between < >. Any words set as such <[ ]> were added then deleted by Baudelaire. In the case of two consecutive words, with the first in square brackets & the second between [ ] or < >, the second word or phrase replaces the first.

Baudelaire's capitalization, as his orthography in general, has been respected, even if at odds with contemporary practice. The aim here was not to contemporize Baudelaire, *Satan forbid*, but to create a translation as close to mid-19th C. English as possible.

For copies of Baudelaire's original manuscripts, see Eugène Crépet's edition of his *Œuvres posthumes* (Quantin, 1887), Philippe Soupault's *Baudelaire* (Rieder, 1931), and tome II of *Œuvres complètes* (Le Club du Meilleur Livre, 1955).

I would like to express my thanks to Genese Grill, Mary Shaw, and Erika Mihálycsa for observations that led to my refining the introduction. Gratitude is especially due to Jean Gatti & Gregory Flanders for their magnanimous efforts in helping me to improve this translation.

BELGIUM STRIPPED BARE

2. I. BEGINNING

Possible titles.

"One must, whatever Danton may say, carry one's country on the soles of one's shoes."

— France appears to be barbarous, when looking from [very] close up: but go to Belgium, and you will be less severe.

— The Thanks that Joubert gave to God.

— Great merit of making a book on Belgium. To be entertaining when speaking of boredom; instructive when speaking of nothing; <to> build on the point of a needle; <to> dance on a loose rope: <to> swim in an [asphaltite] <asphaltite> lake, or in [dorman] dormant water.

To make a sketch of Belgium there is also this advantage: that we make a caricature of the follies of France.

Conspiracy of flatterers against Belgium. Belgium has taken all those compliments seriously.

— Twenty years ago, we were singing the praises of America in this country.

— Why [we do not say] < the French are not telling > the truth about Belgium — [because they don't dare admit that they've been duped] < because, as Frenchmen, they cannot admit that they have been duped. >

— Voltaire's verses on Belgium.

3. TITLES

Grotesque Belgium
The Real Belgium
Belgium Entirely Naked
Belgium Stripped Bare

A Joke of a Capital
A Grotesque Capital
The Capital of Apes
A Capital of Apes

4. BEGINNING

Danton. The Carp and the Rabbit. *America and Belgium*. I wish I had the abilities of ... so many writers of whom I was always jealous. <A certain style,

not the style of Hugo the Belgian author>. Such is my *Lambert*.

Make a Devilish book.

Make an entertaining book on a boring theme. — (The Cabotins)

The loose rope and the asphaltite lake.

A little poem about Amina Boschetti.[1]

A poor man who sees objects of luxury, a sad man who breathes [the odors] of his childhood in the odors of the Church, [so I was] thus I was before Amina.

Amina's arms & legs. The prejudice of thin sylphs.

A joyful feat of strength. Polite gossip — Élisa Guerri. The Gin.

Talent in the Desert.

It is said that Amina is saddened.

She smiles among a people who cannot smile. She flits among a people where each woman could, with a single elephantine paw, crush a thousand eggs.

5. BEGINNING

France is, undoubtedly, a very barbarous country. Belgium also.

Civilization may have taken refuge in some small as of yet undiscovered tribe.

Let us beware of the Parisians' dangerous capacity for generalization.

We have <perhaps> spoken too badly of France.

One must always carry one's country on the soles of one's shoes. It's a disinfectant.

There is fear here of becoming stupid. [Slowness] Atmosphere of somnolence. Universal slowness. (The Fast Train is its symbol.)

The offspring of the Carp & the Rabbit.

The French [prefer] <love best> to deceive [rather] rather than to confess that they have been deceived. French vanity.

6. **BRUSSELS**
   BEGINNING

   Information, useless for the informed.

   The aim of a satyrique piece is to kill two birds with one stone. To make a sketch of Belgium, there is [this first], in addition, the advantage of making a caricature of France.

7. BEGINNING

   France observed from a distance.
   Loathsome books.
   [Letters] (Parisian studies by a non-diplomat.)

8. BEGINNING

   Shall we say that the world has become uninhabitable to me — ?

9. CONSPIRACY OF FLATTERERS AGAINST BELGIUM

   [Press clipping of some fragments from an article published in *Revue britannique* under the title: "Belgian Industry and its Progress."

Belgium has become a subject of observation for those "who are interested in the great social questions of our time and the high aims of political economy. Foreign publicists have commented both on the institutions and on the natural aptitudes that have made the Belgian people so prosperous." Everywhere in Europe, Belgium is offered as an example. And *Revue britannique* was pleased "to echo such deserved praises."]

10. BEGINNING

Make an entertaining work on a thankless subject.
Belgium and the United States, Children spoiled by gazettes.

11. *Epigraph*

Cooper

12. *My Heart Laid Bare*
Notes on *Belgium*
(not categorized) Spleen of Paris
Stances of Defré,[2]
Guide.

13. *Belgium*

[Nullity] Conversational impotence. — I don't like the Belgians. — Why? — Because they don't know French. — Sir, says the Belgian, there are the Hottentots. — Sir, the Hottentots are very far away, and you are very close; besides, I've been told, to be completely honest, that the Hottentots have long been ..... damned. — Why? for not knowing French? — Yes, sir.

14. PHYSIOGNOMY OF THE BELGIANS

[The eye]
The frightened, bulbous, stupid, fixed eye. Apparent dishonesty, simply due to slowness of vision.

Belgians who turn around while walking, and who finally fall to the ground.

Shape of the jaws.
Heaviness of the tongue.
Whistling.
Slow and clumsy pronunciation.

15. BRUSSELS
General impressions
Human physiognomy

The Belgian eye: fat, enormous, staring, insolent (to foreigners).

Innocent eye of a people who cannot see everything in the blink of an eye.

A character [from C] from *Cyrano* says to another: You're so fat that we couldn't beat the entirety of you in a day.

Everything is so [large] vast for the Belgian eye that he needs time to look at it.

The Belgian eye has the innocent insolence of the microscope.

16. *The* bon mot *in Belgium*

In this country, the *bon mot* (for example: *yet another Frenchman who has come to discover Belgium*), generally borrowed from a French vaudevilliste, has a tough life. [Five thousand] One hundred thousand people can use it ten times a day without wearing it out. Such as a piece of musk that keeps its perfume without losing any of its mass. Such as the brandied cherry hanging from the ceiling by a string and licked by a multitude of children but which remains

<long> intact. There is, however, the difference that a smarter child sometimes swallows it, while thousands of Belgians never catch the whole *bon mot*, <or rather swallow it, <without digesting it,> vomit it up, repeat it, *&* swallow it again without disgust, before vomiting it up again with equal indifference.> Happy people! an economical people, moderate in its pleasures! Happy people whose organic constitution is such that it can never [permit] a *debauchery of spirit!*

17.
        Spleen of Paris.
        Odd conversation.
        Let's not offend the Manes.[3]
        The rosary.

   Belgian Civilization.
   The Belgian is very civilized.
   He wears pants, an overcoat, and carries an umbrella, like other men. He gets soused and fucks like the people from beyond Quiévrain. He pretends to have the pox, to resemble [the French] a Frenchman. He knows how to use a fork. He is a liar, <ruthless,> he is cunning, he is very civilized.
   The Amateur of Fine Arts in Belgium.

He listened to me very well, quietly, like an automaton.

[Collected] <Solemn>; then suddenly, with a diplomatic tone,

emerging from a long and surprising state of being drowsy,

which all Belgians share with cows,

with the blink of a provincial merchant,

he says to me: "I believe, *moreover*, that David is on the rise!"

18. BELGIUM
POLITICAL CUSTOMS

"There are, strictly speaking, only two great parties here: the Catholics & the drunkards."
(French Revolutionary brochure whose title escapes me.)

19. BELGIUM
POLITICAL CUSTOMS
[*The Companion of Dumouriez*][4]

"The 5th class (the masses), which uses only beer, brandy, rye, and the solitary amusement of the pipe, has very slow moral fluctuations. Hence the passive character and high opinion of the priests, to which it seems to have granted the exclusive right to think in its place. This seemed so true to me that, after a careful analysis, I saw in it (this people) just two powerful forces for its actions. Those forces are the coin and the host. This people is gentle and submissive; but excited in the name of heaven, or thrust into political metamorphosis, without being taken in by itself. Its fury and its <known> energy can grow to such a degree of intensity that it would become a Bull."

P. Gadolle

The fortune assured by the union of Belgium with France, a very topical idea. 1794 (?) in Guffroy.[5]

20. BELGIUM

BEGINNING

> This sad city where I am,
> It is the abode of ignorance,
> Of torpidity, of boredom,
> Of stupid indifference,
> An old country where obedience,
> Deprived of spirit, is fat with faith.

Voltaire, in Brussels, 1722[6]

The last three words are too much.

21. BEGINNING

[The Prayer of Joubert]
The Gratitude of Joubert.
Should I thank God for having made me French and not Belgian?

22. 2. BRUSSELS

— Physiognomy of the Street.
— First impressions.
— They say that each city, [and that ea] that each country has its own smell. Paris, it's said, smells of sour cabbage. Cape Town smells of sheep. The Orient of musk and carrion.

Brussels smells of black soap. The rooms smell of the black soap with which they [are] have been washed. The beds smell of black soap, which causes insomnia during the first few days. The sidewalks smell of black soap.

— Universal blandness of life. Cigars, vegetables, flowers, cooking, hairstyles, eyes. Everything seems bland, sad, sleepy. Human physiognomy: vague, somber, sleepy <horrible fear of becoming stupid>. The dogs alone are alive. <The Negroes of Belgium.>

— Brussels is much noisier than Paris because of the cobblestones, the fragility and the sonority of the houses, <the narrowness of the streets,> the accent of the people, the pervasive tactlessness, [& finally] the national whistling & the barking of dogs.

— [No] Few sidewalks <or interrupted sidewalks>.
— Terrible cobblestones. — No life in the Street. — Lots of balconies, no one on the balconies. — A city without a river. — No display cases in front of the shops. — *Flânerie* <, so dear to imaginative people,> is impossible.

— Innumerable lorgnettes [on the nose] <. The why —>. — Abundance of Hunchbacks.

— The Belgian face, indistinct, shapeless; bizarre structure of the jaws, menacing stupidity.

— The Belgian gait, crazy & heavy. [Those] They look over their shoulders as they walk.

< The *Spies*, a sign of boredom, curiosity intensified by frustration, by distrust & inhospitality. >

23. GENERAL CHARACTERISTICS. Brussels

The smells of cities. Paris, it's said, smells of sour cabbage. Cape Town smells of sheep. The orient of musk & carrion. Frankfurt...? Brussels smells of black soap.
Laundry. Insomnia caused by the black soap.
Few fragrances.
Not so much stew.

Universal blandness of cigars, vegetables, flowers (spring in arrears, the rainy, heavy, and soft heat of summer), eyes, hair, gaze.

The animals seem sad and sleepy.

Human physiognomy is heavy, puffed up.

Heads like large yellow rabbits, yellowish eyelashes.

They resemble dreaming sheep.

Pronunciation heavy, slurred. The syllables don't emerge from the throat.

The pepper here becomes cucumber.

A chapter on dogs, where the vitality absent elsewhere seems to have taken refuge.

Leashed dogs. (Phrase from Dubois.)

24. BRUSSELS. Physiognomy of the Street

The washing of sidewalks, even when it rains *&* pours. National mania. I saw young girls scrubbing a small area of pavement with a little rag for hours on end.

Sign of imitation, [and sign] and mark above all of a Race not very particular in regards to its choice of amusements.

25. BRUSSELS. GENERAL CHARACTERISTICS CUSTOMS

<Dogs>, the negroes of Belgium.

The sadness of animals. Dogs are no more caressed than women. It's impossible to make them play & to make them frisky. They are then astonished like a prostitute to whom we say: Miss.

But what ardor for work!

I saw a big, mighty man lying in his cart & being dragged up a hill by his dog.

Truly the dictatorship of the savage in a savage land where the male does nothing.

AROUND BRUSSELS

Sparsely populated woods.
Very few songbirds.

26. *Brussels*

First impressions

Brussels, a much noisier city than Paris. — Why?

1. *cobblestones* execrable, destroying the wheels of carriages.

2. *awkwardness, brutality, tactlessness* of the people, causing all kinds of accidents.

(About this awkwardness of the people, don't forget the way that the Belgians walk, — looking at it from another side. — The circuitous paths a civilized man takes to try to avoid bumping into a [bel] Belgian. — A Belgian does not walk, he tumbles.)

3. Universal whistling.

4. Shrill, bawling, foolish character. Howls of the Belgian beast.

Paris, infinitely larger & busier, produces only a vast & vague, velvety buzzing, so to speak.

27. Streets of BRUSSELS

Why Brussels is so noisy:

— special sonority of the cobblestones.

— fragility and vibration of the houses.

— tactlessness of laborers and coachmen.

— [the raucous, drawling voice, the Belgian accent] <the shouting voices of Flemish brutality>.

— the barking of dogs.

— the universal whistle.

BOARDING SCHOOL CHILDREN

Whenever the Belgians [who] <that they> are having fun or are thinking, they [are] always resemble boarding school children — men, women, boys, little girls. —

Even women piss only in a group. They go for a pissing, as Béroalde says.[7]

My fight against a group of ladies from Brussels in Ribote.

28. BRUSSELS. General look of the streets

> No sidewalks, or so few.
> Terribly uneven.
> No gutters.

The way in which the inhabitants bump into each other, and how they carry their canes.

29. CUSTOMS. BRUSSELS

The tic of laughter without cause, especially among women.

Smiling is nearly impossible for them. The muscles of their faces are not flexible enough to make that sweet movement.

GENERAL CHARACTERISTICS

No life in the Street.
Lots of balconies. No one on the balcony.
Little gardens in the backyards of houses.
Everyone at home. Doors closed.

No toilets in the Streets.

No display cases in the shops.

What they lack is a river, which the canals do not replace.

— A city without a river.

And the endless hills make *flânerie* impossible.

30. BRUSSELS
GENERAL EXTERNAL CHARACTERISTICS
CUSTOMS

Lots of balconies. No one on the balcony. Nothing to see in the street.

Everyone at home! (little interior garden)

The complaints of an Italian man.

No display cases in the shops.

Strolling before the shops, that [thing] delight, that education, completely impossible! —

Everyone at home!

31. BRUSSELS
GENERAL CHARACTERISTICS

Many balconies. But no one on the balcony.

A land of homebodies.

Besides, what could they look at in the street?

32. BRUSSELS

Characteristic traits of the Street and of the population.

The lorgnette, with cord, suspended from the nose.

Multitude of vitreous eyes, even among the officers.

An optician tells me that most of the lorgnettes he sells are mere glass. Thus this national lorgnette is nothing more [than a] than a poor attempt at elegance and a [another sign] new sign of the spirit of apishness *&* conformity.

33. BRUSSELS
GENERAL CHARACTERISTICS
EXTERIORS

Comfortable appearance in general. [Cleanliness] Cleanliness of the curtains *&* blinds.

[through]

Flowers in very great quantities. Rooms with a moderately wealthy appearance.

In the back, an overstuffed little garden.

Amazing resemblance between all apartments.

Seen from up close, the luxury is not only monotonous, but trashy.

34. BRUSSELS
GENERAL CHARACTERISTICS

The Belgians are a whistling people, like foolish birds.

They don't whistle tunes.

Vigorous projection of the whistle. My ears pierced.

It's an incurable childhood habit.

Frightening ugliness of the children: lousy, filthy, snotty, ignoble.

Ugliness *&* dirtiness. Even clean, they would still be hideous.

People whistling *&* laughing without cause, with shouts. Sign of idiocy.

All Belgians, without exception, have [empty brains] [brains] empty skulls.

35. BRUSSELS
GENERAL CHARACTERISTICS

The Belgian face, or rather Brusselian.

Chaos.

Shapeless, deformed, rough, heavy, tough, unfinished, cut with a knife.

Angular dentition.

Mouth ill-adapted for the smile.

Laughter exists, it's true, but inept, huge, *with no cause*.

Obscure face without a mien, like that of a cyclops, not a one-eyed cyclops, but a blind one.

Quote the verses of Pétrus Borel.[8] Absence of a mien, terrible thing.

The monstrous thickness of the tongue, among many things, which causes the pronunciation to be mushy *&* wheezy.

36. BELGIUM
BRUSSELS
General physiognomy

Strange look of the mouths in the street and everywhere:

no voluptuous lips;

no commanding lips;

no ironic lips;

no eloquent lips.

Gaping latrines of imbecility.

Gaping cloaca.

Shapeless mouths.

Unfinished faces.

37. BRUSSELS CHARACTERISTICS
GENERAL TRAITS

All Belgian faces have something dark, fierce, or defiant about them, some with the faces of sacristans, others, of savages.

Threatening stupidity.

Maturin's sentence: "It is certain that the gloomiest prospect presents nothing so chilling as the aspect of human faces, in which we try in vain to trace one corresponding expression."[9]

Their gait, at once precipitated, inconsiderate, & indecisive, naturally occupying a lot of space.

Abundance of Hunchbacks.

38. BRUSSELS

Physical features.

Brussels is the country of Hunchbacks, the domain of Rickets.

Why?

Is it the water, is it the beer, is it the squalor of the city and its housing?

In short, it's the same race as in earlier times.

Just as the pisser and the vomitter and the Fairs of Ostades and Teniers still express the joy and the foolishness of the Flemish, so we shall again find in the present life the ankylosed styles of the primitive painters of the North.

39. BRUSSELS
GENERAL TRAITS

The ugly can't understand beauty.

Let us bring together the general ugliness of those people with this other fact: their general hatred of Beauty. Examples: the laughter of the Street and of assemblies before true beauty, — the radical inability of Belgian artists to understand Raphael.

A young writer has recently had an ingenious but not absolutely just viewpoint. The world is going to end. Humanity is decrepit. A Barnum of the future shows the deteriorated men of his time a beautiful, artificially preserved woman from an earlier age. "Eh! what! they say, humanity could be as beautiful as that?" I say that that isn't true. The deteriorated men would admire and call beauty ugliness. Think of those deplorable Belgians.

40. BRUSSELS
GENERAL CHARACTERISTICS
CUSTOMS

The Belgians don't know how to walk. They take up a whole street with their feet & their arms. Having no flexibility, they're unable to get out of the way, to move aside; they strike the obstacle, heavily.

Cold, sly, defiant mien. Expression both fierce and shy. The vague glance, and even when looking you in the face, always indecisive. [Evil] <defiant> race, because it believes it is even weaker than it is.

WOMEN

The woman doesn't exist. The dirty tone of white leukorrhea. And then, since she isn't accustomed to caresses, she can't please. She never tries.

There are females & males. There is no gallantry. — No grooming.

41. *Poor Belgium*
Brussels

Street habits. The Belgian's walk is foolish & heavy.
The Belgians look over their shoulders while walking. It seems as if a foolish curiosity draws their heads back, while an automatic movement pushes

them forward. — A Belgian may make thirty or forty paces, with his head turned backwards, but infallibly a moment comes when he bumps into someone or something. I have beaten many a path to avoid marching Belgians when I walk.

In a crowd the Belgian presses his neighbor forward with his two fists with all his strength. The only solution is to abruptly turn round, giving him, as if by accident, a strong jab to the stomach with your elbow.

42. CUSTOMS
    BRUSSELS

Belgian clumsiness. The Belgians don't know how to walk. *The space a Belgian takes* in THE STREET. It's worse than the French laborers so much sung of by Pierre Dupont.[10]

Clumsiness of Belgian coachmen.

(There are several very steep slopes in Brussels)

They can't give directions.

43. 3. BRUSSELS. CUSTOMS.
    < LIFE, TOBACCO, COOKING, WINES. >

— The question of Tobacco.
  The disadvantages of Liberty.

— The question of cuisine.

No roast meats.

Everything is steamed.

Everything is made with rancid butter (out of economy or taste).

Execrable vegetables (either due to poor quality or to the butter).

No Stews.

Belgian cooks believe that very seasoned food is food doused with salt.

— No fruits. Those from Tournai are exported to England — not to speak of the bread, which is execrable < damp, soggy, burnt >.

— Besides the famous [prejudice] < lie > of Belgian liberty, the lie of Belgian cleanliness, let's add the lie *of everyday life being very cheap.*

Everything is four times more expensive than in Paris, where nothing but the rent is expensive.

— Here, everything is expensive, except the rent.

— You can, it is true, live the Belgian way; [if you] depiction of the diet and hygiene of the Belgians.

— The question of wines. — Wine, curiosity and bric-a-brac object. — Wonderful cellars, *all alike*; expensive *&* heady wines. — The Belgians *display* their wines, yet don't drink them out of taste, but out of vanity.

— Belgium, paradise for traveling wine Salesmen.

— Faro *&* juniper.

44. BRUSSELS

On the question of Tobacco.

45. POOR BELGIUM

A great article on *the question of Cuisine*.
Blandness.
Bread.
Rancid butter.
The vegetables themselves: peas, asparagus, potatœs!
Eggs with black butter.

Absence of fruit.
Absence of hors d'œuvres.

No stews.
The Belgian is no more a gourmand than a Papuan.
His cuisine is disgusting *&* elementary.
But the food merchant .... ?

The question of wine!

46. BRUSSELS
GENERAL TRAITS
COOKING

Mr. Nadar's omelets.

47. BRUSSELS

The question of wines and of wine.

Do Belgians like their wine? Yes, as a bric-a-brac object.

If they could display it without others drinking it and without drinking it themselves, they would be very satisfied.

They drink it, out of vanity, to pretend that they love it.

Always old wines.

The Norman peasant and cider.

48. BRUSSELS

The question of wines.

In public, wine; amongst family, beer. They drink wine *out of vanity*, to look French, but they don't like it.

Always aping and counterfeiting.

The question of bread.
The question of vegetables.
The question of butter.
Comestible merchants.

Advice to the French.

49. BRUSSELS
GENERAL CHARACTERISTICS
CUSTOMS

[History of]

Universal economy.

History of the gentleman who doesn't want to pay for pickles at Horton's.

Faro, 2 *sous* 3 *centimes*.

Frenetic love of *centimes*.

Chairs without back rails.

The habit of serving drinks to the mark, as if the innkeeper was responsible for watching over the drinker's outrageousness.

Frightening drunkenness of the people. Cheapness of drinking. Faro and juniper.

Bourgeois cellars, marvelously opulent. The wines age there.

50. *Cooking article*
Drink of the Brusselians

Faro is taken from the great latrine, the Senne; it's a drink extracted from the excrement of the [Se] city *&* subjected to a filtering device. Thus, for centuries, the city drinks its urine.

51. 4. CUSTOMS
WOMEN AND LOVE

— No *women*, no *love*.

— Why?

— No gallantry among men, no modesty among women. — Modesty, something prohibited, or something for which no need is felt.

Broad portrait of the Flemish woman, or at least of the Brabant woman (putting aside, for a moment, the Walloon woman).

General type, analogous to that of sheep *&* rams. The smile, impossible, because of the recalcitrance of the muscles, [of the] and the structure of the teeth and jaws.

The complexion, the hair; the legs, the breasts, full of tallow; the feet, horror !!!

In general, swelling like a swamp. Precocity of plumpness.

The stench of the women (anecdotes).

— [The] obscenity of Belgian Ladies. — Anecdotes about latrines.

Refer, in regards to love, to the garbage of the old Flemish painters. The sex life of sixty-year olds. The people haven't changed.

— Females, yes. — Women, no.

— Belgian prostitution.

— Extracts from regulations.

52. BRUSSELS

The General Woman

Nose of pulcinella, forehead of a [sheep] ram, eyelids like onion-skin, colorless & empty eyes, a monstrously small mouth, or simply an absence of mouth (neither word, nor kiss!), a retracted jaw, flat feet, with elephantine legs (like wooden beams on boards), a lilac complexion, and with all that the fatuity & peacocking of a pigeon.

52r. BRUSSELS

Women in the Street.
Their feet.
Their calves.
Their stench.

If you cede the sidewalk to them, as they are accustomed to cede it to men, they come down from the sidewalk at the same time as you, [and] they collide with you, and thank you for your good intentions by calling you a lout.

Description of some Belgian women. — The nose, the eyes, the throat. Rubens' portraits.

52v. Ink.
Scissors.
Moist bread as sealing wax.

54. BRUSSELS
GENERAL CHARACTERISTICS
CUSTOMS

The Belgians walk in a manner at once furious *&* indecisive, like the carriages driven by their detestable coachmen.

WOMEN

The women walk with their feet turned in. Large, flat feet.

The large arms, large breasts, and large calves of the women.

A marshy force.

55. CUSTOMS
BRUSSELS
THE WOMEN

A remedy for love, expression of Louis XIII.
Here, no merit for man to be chaste.
Priapus would become sad.
Both genders stand apart.

Among men, no gallantry.
Among women, no coquetry.
No resistance, no shame.
Among men, no glory, no conquest, no merit.
All blond, bland, with the blue or grey eyes of sheep, which bulge out.
A Kaffir would be an Angel here.
Curvaceousness and precocity of the young girl. Adipose precociousness.
Vegetables reared in marshy ground.
Women don't know how to walk. — No grooming for the world.
Some Frenchwomen — kept, but very sad. — Take some strange notes on the rules of prostitution. —

56. *Poor Belgium*
 Women

There are females here, but no women. No gallantry. No coquetry. No shame.
Modesty is a Parisian trait that isn't accepted, either because it's prohibited, or because no one feels the need for it.

57. BRUSSELS
   WOMEN
   LOVE

> Love is remarkable by its absence. What one calls love here is pure animal [oper] gymnastics, which I don't have to describe to you.

> Vomiting lovers.

> The young [girl], a paper merchant, filled the shop with a stench. (The old English woman suffers from *Delirium tremens*.)

> The girl breaks out into laughter at the man who asks her the way, or replies: *Gott for dum!* ....

58. BRUSSELS
General traits

> The Belgian woman. No gallantry, no shame.
> The pissing & shitting of Belgian ladies.
> The Belgian mother on her latrine, [plays with her] (door open) plays with her child and smiles at her neighbors.
> Prodigious love of excrement found in old paintings. It was indeed their homeland that those painters depicted.

In a small street, six Belgian ladies pissing, barring the passage, some standing, the others crouching, all finely done up.

The cleanliness of Belgian women. Difficult to avoid the stench of a Belgian lady, & of her daughter (Montagne-de-la-Cour), even in the street.

59. CUSTOMS

I have never been able to make it clear to a Belgian that gallantry constitutes a large part of the education that a French mother gives to her son.

— The Belgians believe that gallantry means bestiality!

>Sunday, Nov. 27
>*Belgian independence*

>Sophocles & Virgil
>Lord Duruy

60. 5. CUSTOMS

>Belgian crudeness (even *among the officers*).
>
>The amenities of colleagues.
>
>Tone of Belgian criticism & journalism.

Belgian vanity wounded.

Belgian vanity in Mexico.

Baseness and domesticity.

Belgian morality. Monstrosity in crime.

Orphans & old people in adjudication.

(The Flemish party. Victor Joly. His legitimate accusations against the spirit of Apishness) (to be placed elsewhere).

61. Brussels: Politesse
[Press clipping about the absence of politesse among the "inferior classes." In a marginal note, Baudelaire counters that every class suffers from the absence of politesse.]

62. Belgian Patriotism
[Press clipping from *Espiègle* (May 1865) about Théâtre de la Monnaie's production of *Le Captif*, a comic opera by Mr. Cormon about Cervantes, with music by Edouard Lassen.[11] The article speaks of the complete and well-deserved success of the piece, which is reported with all the more pleasure since Lassen is Belgian. The writer is disavowed as having

nothing to do with the success since the libretto is insignificant, hence "it is a miracle that Lassen found in it the matter for such a charming score."]

63. Universal crudity, in every class
    Exploit of five officers
    [Press clipping from *Gazette belge* (Nov. 3, 1865) about a police captain & four of his officers assaulting Mr. Verhulst, the director of *Nouvelliste de Gand*, in his office because of an article they found defamatory.]

64. Belgian logic
    [Press clipping from *Gazette belge* (Nov. 5, 1865) about the resignation of Col. Vandersmissen & the officers of the Belgian Expeditionary Force for their involvement in a conspiracy to annex Mexico to the USA. Senior Mexican officials were alleged to be part of the plot, resulting in the arrest of 100 people & Emperor Maximilian being obliged to leave the capital. On the article, Baudelaire writes: *The officers giving their resignation, it is clear that Maximilian only has to leave. Belgian logic.*]

65. Expedition of [Belgi] Mexico
 Belgian Vanity
 [Press clipping from *Gazette belge* (Nov. 5, 1865) about the disaffection of the Belgian officers serving in Mexico. The correspondent complains of him & his officers being poorly rewarded for their troubles.]

66. CONFORMITY
 BASENESS
 DOMESTICITY
 [Press clipping from *Sancho* (August 21, 1864) about procuring government favors only for Freemasons and Solidarists. "Will we return to those fine days of the Dutch government, when petitioners put aside their requests: 'The applicant has the honor of belonging to the reformed religion'?" In the margin, CB writes: *Proof that this people has always had a domestic character, a* conformist *character*.]

67. Family feelings
 No soul
 [Press clipping from *Gazette belge* (Sept. 23, 1865) about a father selling two of his children, aged 4 & 8, to a saltimbanque.]

68. Family feelings
　　Morality (Ardennes)
　　[Press clipping from *Écho de Bruxelles* (Aug. 5, 1864) about a case of incest and infanticide denoting the culprits' incredible cruelty. Jean-Baptiste Périn and his sister were accused of killing a newborn child. After strangling the baby, they boiled it, fed it to a pig, then threw the remaining bones into a fire. The sister is acquitted & her brother is sentenced to forced labor for life.]

69. BRUSSELS
　　Morality

　　　　Criminality & [fierc] immorality of Belgium.
　　　　Here a crime is fiercer, stupider than elsewhere.
　　　　Rape of a child of [twelve] ‹fourteen› months.
　　　　Prodigious immorality of the priests. The priests are recruited from the hideous race of the peasants.

　　　　Dog eaten alive. For 20 francs.

70. BELGIUM. CUSTOMS
　　CRIMES: DRUNKENNESS

　　　　Particularly savage & bestial character of Belgian drunkenness.

[observe...]

A father is drunk. He castrates his son.

Observe in this crime not only the ferocity, but the manner of the crime.

A Belgian can only [joke] <banter> about or make fun of the sexual organs. True obsession.

71. *Crudeness*
Belgian Bestiality

> The man who gets rich in fairs by eating live dogs. Audience of women and children.

72. *The Flemish Section*
[Press clipping from *Sancho, Journal du Dimanche. Revue des Hommes et des Choses*, № 14 (May 1865).]

Joly's patriotism

Very legitimate
accusations against
the spirit of
BELGIAN APISHNESS

The above statements are repeated on the clipping. The following variant of CB's, "*Spirit of imitation in Belgium*," is repeated on the second clipping, an article titled "The Outlawed Flemish Language," in which Joly protests the Brussels City Council, which has just declared that "the Flemish language is not permitted to appear on any public monument in the capital," & joins the protests about this made in the House of Representatives to the Minister of the Interior. Baudelaire has marked in black & red various parts of the lengthy article that concern the foreign influence over every domain of Belgian culture & society, from the press to the arts, philosophy, & language, and the Belgians propensity to ever so freely adopt such influence. Joly himself denounces this apishness as the work of denationalization, which every day destroys the lineament of Belgium's national physiognomy by declaring that the language of its fathers is unworthy of standing beside that of its eternal enemies. "We have the right to be astonished that Mr. Anspach, the honorable burgomaster of the capital, whose eminently patriotic sentiments we have so often applauded, has not protested against the inconceivable avidity gratuitously made by our Flemish people and do not understand how much we are clearing the way for the rectifiers of borders, by using their language in our public acts, in the debates of our courts, our chambers, in our theaters, in our public & private relations."

[The second press clipping concerns the public auctioning of orphans and old people as a form of white slave trading. In the margin, CB writes: *Belgian immorality. Orphans and the elderly in adjudication. Marvel that can only take place in a soulless people. Ferocity, stupidity, greed, bestiality together.*]

73. CUSTOMS

The Belgian brain

Belgian Conversation

It is as difficult to define the [Bru] Belgian character as it is to classify the Belgian in the rank of beings.

He is an ape, *but* he is a mollusk.

An astonishing heaviness with a prodigious [versatility] <absent-mindedness>. It's easy to oppress him, as history notes; it's almost impossible to crush him.>

To judge him, let's focus on certain ideas: apishness, counterfeiting, conformity, [hatr], hateful impotence, and we could classify all the facts under those different titles.

Their vices are counterfeit.

The Belgian *gandin*.[12]

The Belgian patriot.

The Belgian slaughterer.

The Belgian freethinker, whose main characteristic is to *believe* that you *don't believe what you're saying*, since he doesn't understand it.

< Counterfeits of French impiety *&* dirty jokes. >

Presumption *&* fatuity. — Familiarity. Portrait of a Wallon dodo brain.

Terrified of the spiritual life. History of Valbezen in Antwerp.[13] — Terrified of laughter. — Boisterous laughter without cause. — A touching story is told, the Belgian bursts out laughing, to make believe that he understood. — They are Ruminants who digest nothing.

— And yet, there is a Boeotia in Belgium, Poperinghe.[14]

74. BRUSSELS
Customs
Morality

The Belgian character is not very well defined. It drifts between [the oyster] <the mollusk> *&* the ape.

75. BRUSSELS
Moral characters

It's difficult to assign the Belgian a place in the rank of beings. However, we can affirm that it must be classified between the Ape and the Mollusk. There's plenty of room there.

76. BRUSSELS
GENERAL TRAITS

The Belgian knows how to eat his soup by himself, with a spoon. He even knows how to use forks and knives, though his awkwardness testifies that he would rather tear into the prey with his teeth & his dirty claws.

77. IGNORANCE,
VANITY,
& BELGIAN VILLAINY

I've seen extraordinary things in Brussels.

Architects who are ignorant of the history of architecture.

Painters who have never looked at an engraving after Raphael, and who paint a picture based on a photograph.

Women who insult you if you offer them a bouquet.

[Others] Ladies who, while they are *officiating* there, leave the latrine door open.

Counterfeit gandins who have violated all women.

[Fre] Thinkers who are afraid of ghosts.

Patriots who want to massacre all the French (those who put their right arm in a sling to pretend that they <have> fought).

And finally (this is the bulk of the nation) a crowd of people who tell you when you say to them: God … : you cannot believe what you say. — Imply: because I don't understand.

And officers who gang up to assault a journalist in his office.

78. BRUSSELS
GENERAL CHARACTERISTICS
CONVERSATION

Amazing Belgian presumption, in every order. — Someone has done something — a book, a picture, a brilliant action; —, I could do it as well (it's obvious (!)), therefore I am his equal.

79. BRUSSELS
GENERAL CHARACTERISTICS
CUSTOMS

When a Belgian addresses ten people, he always speaks to one person, even turning his back to the rest of the group to whom he is speaking.

A Belgian never gives way to a woman on the sidewalk.

So far I've only once seen in a theater a man trying to attract the attention of an audience through his attitude and mien.

Though he wore light-colored clothes & an overcoat, with rings over amethyst colored gloves, no one noticed him.

Besides, the Belgians always appear badly dressed, although they try very hard to dress well. Everything looks bad on them.

The most brilliant nature would be extinguished here in universal indifference. Impossibility of a vain existence.

Here, about art, as in small towns, one cannot say: *Bis repetita placent*.[15]

80. BRUSSELS
   GENERAL TRAITS

The contempt of Belgians for famous men.

[Everyone] Their familiarity with the famous man. They would immediately tap his belly and make familiar with him as if they had rolled around together as children in the dust and filth of the Marolles.[16]

Everyone is convinced that he will do as much since *he is a man. Homo sum, nihil humani a me alienum puto.*[17] New translation.

81. BRUSSELS
    CUSTOMS

Universal boastfulness, when it comes to women, money, duels, etc. ...

Necessity for each man to boast of himself in a country where no one challenges you to a duel.

Besides, no one deceives anyone, since everyone knows that his neighbor is as much a liar as himself. At most he believes half of what is stated as fact!

Here, woe to Modesty. It cannot be [...] <understood or> rewarded. If a man of merit says: "I have done very little," one comes to the obvious conclusion that he has done nothing!

82. BRUSSELS
   CUSTOMS
   GENERAL TRAITS

With so much heaviness, no fixity. A great ponderousness with an astonishing versatility.

Velocity proportionate to ponderousness. It's always the herd of sheep, to the right, to the left, to the north, to the south, who rush together as a mass.

I have never seen a Belgian daring to stand up, not to a thousand, but just to ten, and say: "You are mistaken, — or, you are unfair." These people only think as a mass.

Also, there is nothing here that is more fashionable, nor more visible, nor more honorable, than the low blow. The *Vae victis* has never found such keen supporters. That's why, since this people has always been conquered, I have the right to tell them joyfully: "*Vae victis*."[18]

83. Wallon

> A little portrait of the *Wallon dodo brain*.
> Turbulent,
> indiscreet,
> [insolent]
> insolent,

conquering the world,

& rethinking Napoléon's plans for the campaign.

Agitated,

telling you: you don't believe what you say.

The Walloon especially is the true caricature of the Frenchman, not the Fleming.

Often wobbly, clubfooted, or hunchbacked.

The Walloons, nursery of lawyers.

84. BRUSSELS
GENERAL TRAITS

To abhor the mind.

History of Mr. de Valbezen, a frivolous man in Antwerp.

85. BRUSSELS
GENERAL TRAITS

The Belgians hate justified laughter; they never laugh when there's reason to. But they *burst out* laughing without cause.

"The weather's fine, don't you think?"
And they burst out laughing.

86. BRUSSELS
GENERAL CHARACTERISTICS

>   About the [*natura morte*] <wildlife> painters,
>   or the eyes of dreaming sheep, or the abhorrence of the mind,
>   the Belgians are *Ruminants* who digest nothing.

87. BRUSSELS
GENERAL CHARACTERISTICS

>   For Brussels, Poperinghe is a Boeotia.
>   But do you Belgians even understand the concept of Comparison or Superlative?

88. 7. CUSTOMS   BRUSSELS
      (suite)

>   Small town mentality
>
>   Gossip.
>   <Jealousies. Slander. Enjoyment of the misfortune of others.>
>
>   Results of idleness & disability.

89. BRUSSELS
GENERAL CHARACTERISTICS
CUSTOMS

Small town mentality.

Belgian defiance. Belgian gossip. Belgian defamation. They called me a spy.
A spy means a man who doesn't think like us.
18th C. synonym: pederast.

90- BRUSSELS
90A. CUSTOMS

Small town curiosity.

If the taste for allegories returned to literature, the poet would not find a more appropriate place than Brussels for *The Temple of Calumny*.

A Belgian whispers in your ear: "Don't frequent that one there. He's a rogue." And that guy says: "Don't frequent that one there. He's a scoundrel." — And so on, everyone, about each other.

But they don't fear bad associations, for they see each other, tolerate each other, and mutually interact with each other, although the entire nation is comprised only of scoundrels, — if we are to believe them.

When I felt myself [defamed *&*] slandered, I wanted to put an end to that national passion, as far as I was concerned *&*, poor fool that I am! I used irony.

To all those who asked me why I stayed so long in Belgium (because they don't like it when foreigners stay too long), I answered confidentially that I was an informant.

And they believed me!

I told others that [I was] I had exiled myself from France because I had committed crimes of such an [a very] unspeakable nature, but I had hoped that, thanks to the appalling corruption of the French regime, I would soon be amnestied.

And they believed me!

Exasperated, I then declared that I was not only a murderer, but a pederast. [The result of] This revelation brought about a completely unexpected result: Belgian musicians concluded that Mr. Richard Wagner was a pederast.

For the idea of a man praising another man in a disinterested way cannot enter [into] beneath a Belgian skull.

91. BRUSSELS
MORAL CHARACTERISTICS

Small town mentality

The idleness of the Belgians renders them very fond of news, gossip, slander, etc.

A village curiosity drives them to the pier to see who is coming.

Few people rejoice as much as they do in the misfortunes that befall others.

(Emerson's thought about the friends of one sick in bed.)[19]

92. BRUSSELS
GENERAL TRAITS

Small town spirit

The Belgians are very defiant. No one on the balcony. You ring, someone opens a door, they look at you as if you are a representative of the people that are coming to claim the remainder of a subsidy.

I passed for an Informant.

I [said] added that I was a Jesuit and a pederast. And they believed me, so stupid are those people!

93. BRUSSELS
CUSTOMS

Indiscretion.
Curiosity.

Small town mentality.

A spirit, close to the gossiping and calumniating spirit, urges the Belgians to listen at doors, to make holes in doors.

Arthur and the concierge.

---

94. BRUSSELS
GENERAL CHARACTERISTICS
CUSTOMS

Small town mentality

Conversation. Abhorrence of the Mind.
Laughter without cause.
Gossip.
The defamation continues.
The dishonor or ruin of a neighbor is always being announced.

When a neighbor is ruined, even if he is the most honest man in the world, everybody runs away from him, for fear of being asked a favor.

Poverty, great dishonor.

Petty city,
  petty minds,
  petty feelings.

95. BRUSSELS
GENERAL CHARACTERISTICS
CUSTOMS

>Belgian curiosity.

>Small town mentality.

>If you stay here for a while, everyone says to [you] you: Monsieur is an expatriate, I guess?

>It's difficult for them to understand that one may remain here *for pleasure*, and live with them voluntarily.

>I always want to answer: yes. Sir, because I've murdered my father, & I've eaten him, [totally raw] without boiling him.

>But they would believe me.

>The Belgian is like the Russian — he is afraid of being studied. He wants to hide his wounds.

96. 8. BRUSSELS
CUSTOMS (continued)

>>Spirit of obedience & conformity.

>>Spirit of association.

>>Innumerable societies. <(A remainder of Corporations.)>

>>The individual: too lazy to think.

>>By coming together, individuals excuse themselves from thinking <individually>.

< The Society of the Joyous. >

A Belgian cannot think he is happy if he doesn't see other people becoming happy through the same process.

< He cannot be happy *by himself*. >

97. BRUSSELS

To bring this closer to the Belgian Nothingness in conversation, the imbecilic laughter, and so on.

SPIRIT OF OBEDIENCE AND CONFORMITY

[I would not believe myself happy]

— If you believe you had found happiness, would you not feel the need to share the recipe?

— No.

— I would — I would not believe that I am happy if I did not see other men living in the same way as myself. *I thus prove my happiness.*

— Such were the speeches of a Belgian who, without provocation on my part, clung to me for four hours in order to tell me that he was very rich, that he owned many oddities, that he was married, that he had traveled, that he often had sea-sickness, that he had fled from Paris on account of the cholera, that he owned a factory in Paris where <all> the foremen were decorated, — and all because of that, hoping to get rid of him, I told him that happiness existed for me only in solitude.

98. BELGIUM
STREET CUSTOMS

The Belgians think only in groups

(freemasons, freethinkers, *societies* of all kinds)
and they amuse themselves only in groups

(amusement societies, societies for future finch blinders)[20]

(little girls locking arms; — likewise little boys, men, and women).

[They will stick togeth]

Both the men and women piss only in groups.

Groups of women that attacked me, and which I managed to get rid of thanks to my cigar.

99. BRUSSELS
GENERAL TRAITS

Love of Belgians for societies, semi-societies, quarters of societies .... Infinite division.

Disciplinary way to have fun, to cry, to rejoice, to pray. — Everything is done the Prussian way.

In sum, that demonstrates the inability of the individual to cry, to pray, and to amuse himself alone.

Old remnants of feudal stupidities: oaths, lineages, corporations, confraternities, nations, trades.

Van der Noot still reigns.[21]

(Curious misunderstanding between the two revolutions, the Brabant and the French.)

100. BRUSSELS
CUSTOMS

There is no people more fit for conformity than the Belgian people. Here they think in groups, they play in groups, they laugh in groups. [They get together] < [set themselves] > [for]. The Belgians form societies to come to an opinion. Hence there is no group of people who feel more astonishment or contempt [for people] than those whose opinion does not conform to theirs. Then it [their] is impossible [for them to conceive] for a Belgian to believe that a man believes what he does not believe. Thus, any dissident is in bad faith.

I know very little about Belgian Catholics. I believe them to be just as stupid, just as bad, and above all just as lazy as Belgian atheists.

— Proof of the spirit of obedience and laziness of the Belgians:

— "Since you have no mass book, why are you going to Church?"

101. BRUSSELS
GENERAL CHARACTERISTICS
CUSTOMS

> Love of societies.
> Love of corporations (Remains of the Middle Ages).
> The Freemasons.
> They think in common. That is, they don't think.
> *India*: burning love of ranks, presidencies, decorations, militarism (civic guard).
> For the smallest success, all ranks in every order, all distinctions come to you at once.
> A little failure & you are no longer of value. You lose everything: you tumble down every scale.

102. 9. BRUSSELS
CUSTOMS

> The Spies.
> Belgian cordiality.
> Lack of deference.
> < Belgian rudeness again. >
>
> The *Gallic salt* of the Belgians.
> Pisser and vomitter. < National statues, which I find symbolic. >
> Excremental jokes.

103. CUSTOMS
BRUSSELS

Belgian cordiality is expressed by the *spyhole*, which clearly indicates that the inhabitant is bored, and that he is not disposed to receive everyone who knocks.

It is expressed by the absence of lighters to ignite cigars. One can only light one's cigar in the place where [they buy them] it is bought.

— By the bad mood of the people to whom one asks one's way. (*God damn! Would you give me some fucking peace?*)

Some will perhaps consent to give you directions; but they are so clumsy that you will understand nothing.

"Sir, first you go that way, and then you will take the avenue, and then you turn toward ……" [being] naming [rightly] <sometimes> the localities that you would need to know to understand them.

"To the right … to the left" an unknown lingo.

104. BRUSSELS
GENERAL CHARACTERISTICS
CUSTOMS

Everyone at home. [Great fortunes.] Nobody on the balcony. The spyhole. The little patch of garden.

Great fortunes. Great savings.

Notes from Malassis. — The King brushes his hat; the rain will spread over the dust. Several millions of men brush their hats & dust their shoulders.

The Belgian worship of their hats. The Belgians love their hats like the peasant of Pierre Dupont loves his oxen.[22]

Matches are equally precious objects. They must be spared.

Chairs without back rails.

Dubois' word on dogs (don't bring your dog, it would be humiliated to see its kind dragging carts. — At least, Monsieur, we don't muzzle them here). Beautiful chapter to write on those vigorous dogs, on their zeal & pride. You might say that they want to [to be compared to] humiliate horses.

105. CUSTOMS
BRUSSELS

"Scratch a civilized Russian," said Bonaparte, "and you will find a Tartar."

This is true even for the most charming Russians that I have known.

Scratch a Belgian prince and you will find a lout.

106. CUSTOMS
BRUSSELS

> Roughness in street customs.
>
> — They don't give way to women on the sidewalk.
>
> — A French workman is an aristocrat to a prince of this country.
>
> Roughness of joking.
>
> The *Gallic salt* of the Belgians. My abhorrence of the famous *Gallic salt*.
>
> French Shit and Belgian shit, two forms of the same kind of joke.
>
> *The man who pisses. The vomitter.*
>
> This coarseness is seen in love. Even in paternal love. The naked asses of Jordæns. That is in Flemish life.
>
> This is seen in political life. Examples taken from newspapers.
>
> This is seen in the clergy. The clergy is stupid *&* provocative.

107. 10. BRUSSELS
CUSTOMS (continued)

> Belgian slowness and laziness <; in socialites, in employees, in workers.>
>
> — Torpor <and complication> [of the adm] of the administrations. —
>
> The post office. — The Telegraph. <, the Warehouse.> <Administrative stories.>

108. BRUSSELS
GENERAL TRAITS

> Belgian sluggishness.

> The idleness of the Belgians.
> They wake up late.
> Even the salesmen don't know what work is.
> A moneychanger takes me for a beggar.

109. BRUSSELS
Heaviness

> ### ADMINISTRATIVE IDLERS
> Interminable deliberations.
> *About everything.*

> Belgian idleness.
> A well digger falls during a landslide.
> Proclamations. Search for workmen. Calls.
> A few days pass. Sunday rest is observed, despite the [command] apologues of Jesus Christ.
> Finally they find the corpse. Then they seek to prove that the man suffocated to death at the very beginning.

110. BRUSSELS
GENERAL CHARACTERISTICS

> The Postal Law.
> The Telegraph.

110. BRUSSELS
GENERAL CHARACTERISTICS
CUSTOMS

> To make a counterpart to the modesty of *L'Espiègle* (our women *&* our sisters),
> the modesty of the Telegraph.

Charpentier	100	Hotel	100
My mother	200	Jousset	600
Villemessant	200	Jeanne	50
		Me	50

112. 11. BRUSSELS CUSTOMS
(continued)

> Belgian morality. <The merchants. Glorification of success.>
> Money.
> The painter who would deliver Jefferson Davis over.[23]
> Universal <*&* reciprocal> distrust, sign of general immorality.

A Belgian can't see a good motive for any action, even a good one.

Crookedness in business (anecdotes).

The Belgian is always inclined to rejoice over the misfortune of others. Besides, it represents [an object] a subject of conversation in and of itself.

The general passion for calumny. I've been the victim of it several times.

General avarice. < Everyone is a salesman, even the rich. >

< Great fortunes. No charity. It seems that there is a conspiracy to keep the people in misery and hebetude. >

Hatred of Beauty, to accompany their hatred of the mind.

Not conforming, that is the great crime.

113. *Poor Belgium*
    General traits

Belgian morality.

Here, there are no [profe] professional thieves. But this lack is largely compensated for by universal crookedness.

Thus in states where [prosperity] legal prostitution does not exist, all women are venal.

114. BRUSSELS
GENERAL CHARACTERISTICS
CUSTOMS

In a country where everyone is defiant, it is obvious that everyone is [guilty] a thief.

115. BRUSSELS
CUSTOMS

Apply to the Belgians the passage from Emerson concerning the opinion of the Yankees on *Cobden* and *Kossuth*. — (*The Conduct of Life*)

Then, about [Lizt] Liszt.....
A Belgian never supposes a good motive.
He will persist in discovering a bad one, because he can only have a bad one himself.

116. BRUSSELS
CUSTOMS

> General crookedness.
> Beware the Jews!
> Beware especially the German-Russians!
> What is the German-Russian.
> Some fine examples of Belgian crookedness.

These people, moreover, are used to stealing from one another, and the victor is held in higher esteem for it.

117. BRUSSELS

Moral characteristics

The Belgian is incommunicable [to you], like a woman, because he has nothing to communicate to you, and <he> you are incommunicable to [y] him, because of his impenetrability. <— Nothing as mysterious, deep, and brief as Nothingness. —>

His hatred of the stranger. How he hates and despises the French! Being idle and [unoccupied] <envious>, he has a perpetual need for slander.

Don't be afraid to afflict him by telling him the truth about himself. If he is able to read, he doesn't.

No one is more inclined to rejoice in the misfortune of others.

Universal barbarism *&* vulgarity, without exception, with the lively affectation of civilized [of appar] manners. *Manners* !!!

118. BRUSSELS
    CUSTOMS

> Hostile atmosphere.
>
> The mien and the face <of> the enemy, everywhere, everywhere.
>
> Slander, theft, etc. ... However, in the early days, bestial curiosity, [with protestations of friendship] <similar to that of ducks who at the slightest noise flock as a mass to the shore>.
>
> The prejudice of Belgian hospitality.
>
> Advice to the French who wish to suffer as little as possible.

119. BRUSSELS
    GENERAL CHARACTERISTICS

> Belgian avarice. One-tenth of the income is spent. The remainder is capitalized.
>
> Delacroix's drawings.

120. *Poor Belgium*

> Insensate race — hatred of Beauty.
>
> Belgian Modesty. — Belgian Dandyism.
>
> In Belgium one senses the enemy everywhere.

Tyranny of the human face, tougher than elsewhere. The astonished, stupefied eye of man, woman, and child.

— Oh! That gentleman, how stupid he looks!

— Effect that a beautiful woman would produce in Brussels. Analysis of the hatred or hilarity caused by Beauty. Beauty is rare. History of Mrs. Muller. — French scoundrel. — Here everyone is a scoundrel.

— On the modesty of Belgian women. The pissers of Rue du Singe. The History of Latrines, open doors. — Little girls.

— The Belgians pretend not to know Flemish; but the proof that they know it is that they harangue their servants in Flemish.

121. 12. CUSTOMS (cont'd)

The prejudice of Belgian cleanliness. What it consists of.

< Successful trades. Launderers, ceiling plasterers. Bad trades. Bath houses. >

Clean things in Belgium.
Poor neighborhoods.
Begging.

122. BRUSSELS
GENERAL CHARACTERISTICS

Among the dirty things:
The Senne,
which could not, since its waters are
so opaque, reflect a single ray of the most blazing sun.

[Sanita]
Sanitation of the Senne.
The only way is to divert it, and prevent it from passing through Brussels, where it serves as a drain to the Latrines.

123. BRUSSELS
CUSTOMS

BELGIAN CLEANLINESS. Great impression of whiteness. Pleasant at first. And then unpleasant. Strange colors: light pink *&* light green.

Clean things: parquet floors, curtains, stoves, facades, rest rooms.

Dirty things: the human body *&* the human soul. (As for perfumes, the eternal black soap.)

Ceiling-plasterers. — Incredible industry. Perhaps painting buildings with bad taste is necessary in this climate.

They water their plants when it rains. —

BELGIAN COOKING. Absent in the Restaurants, — or rather, no Restaurants. Bad bread, for gourmands. — The way to console yourself: read a cookbook. — No mistress, read a book about love.

On the whole, I'm wrong. There is Flemish cooking; but it is not found outside the home.

No roasted meats.

124. BRUSSELS
GENERAL TRAITS

Ugliness & misery.

About prostitution.

Misery, which in all countries softens the heart of the philosopher with such ease, can here only inspire the most irresistible disgust in him, as the face of the poor man is so [permanently] <originally> marked by incurable vice & baseness!

Childhood, beautiful almost everywhere else, is here hideous, infected, mangy, filthy, shitty.

Just take a look at the poor districts, and see the naked children roll around in excrement. However, I [don't] believe that they [don't] eat it.

    The old woman herself, the sexless being, who everywhere else has the great merit of inspiring compassion without moving the senses, retains [everything] on her face [all the horrors of] <all the ugliness and all the stupidity with which> the young woman was marked in the maternal womb. She therefore inspires neither politeness nor respect nor tenderness.

125. 13. BELGIAN ENTERTAINMENT

    Sinister & icy character.
    Lugubrious silence.
    Spirit of conformity.
    They only have fun in groups.
    The carnival in Brussels. <Everyone hops in place
                       & in silence.
                       No one
                       offers a drink to
                       his dance partner. >

    Barbarism of children's games.
    The Vaux Hall.
    The Casino.

Le Théâtre Lyrique.
Le Théâtre de la Monnaie.
The French Vaudeville theaters.
Mozart at the Théâtre du Cirque.

Ball games.
Archery contests.

Working class dances.

The Julius Langenbach troupe (no success, because it had talent).

How I made a whole room applaud a ridiculous dancer.

126. BRUSSELS
GENERAL TRAITS

Multitude of parties.
Everything is a pretext for a party.
Street Fairs.
Triumphal arches for all the victors.
The Publicity Office and the latrines.

127. BRUSSELS
CUSTOMS, PLEASURES

At a concert, the Belgian accompanies the melody with his foot or cane, to make believe that he understands it.

128. BRUSSELS
GENERAL CHARACTERISTICS
CUSTOMS

They listen with attention to serious music,
    with anxiety to dirty jokes.

To make clear that they feel the rhythm, they strike the floor with their canes.

Each concert has a French part; they are afraid, [it is tr] it is true, of being French, but they are afraid of not looking French.

129. PLACES OF ENTERTAINMENT
BRUSSELS

There aren't any.

A ball at *La Louve*.

Majestic dance, but danced by bears. A kind of pavan, of which a choreographer could make a charming thing. Some dance of ancient origin. (The Belgians don't offer refreshments to their dance partners.)

Vaux Hall *&* Zoological Garden.

<The more than pitiful pots.>

The gelid reaction of audiences.

It [fears] does not applaud, in fear, perhaps of getting it wrong.

Théâtre de la Monnaie. Empty room, coldness of the artists, the orchestra, and the public.

Théâtre Lyrique. (They should put a sign at the doorway, as they do on churches: *No dogs in the Temple!*)

Queen Crinoline, a novelty for me as an *Epimenides*.[24]

---

127. BRUSSELS
    POPULAR PLEASURES
    MASKED BALLS

> *More narrow space for*
> *the obedient herd.*
>
> *One could be buried*
> *more cheerfully.*

Deathly silence.
The music itself is *silent*.
They dance funereally.
A masked ball resembles the interment of a free thinker.

The women cannot dance because their [knotted] femurs & the necks of their femurs are knotted together. Their legs are like sticks carved out of wooden planks.

Men! Oh! [French] caricature of [France] France!

The costumes. — Percale dominœs. — Calico packages. Crooks more heinous than any known crook. Hideous animality. — Ah! such hideous things, the barbarous Monkeys!

Tolerate two thousand types of absolute Ugliness!

131. CONCERTS
    ORCHESTRA

Bitter sound of German Brass.

132. CUSTOMS
BRUSSELS

The barbarism of children's games.
Birds fastened by the leg with string, tied to a stick.
A friend of mine cuts the string and gets an earful.
The Street of Finches, in Namur. All eyes poked out.

133. 14. EDUCATION

Universities of the State or the Commune.
Free University.
High schools.
No Latin, no Greek.
No philosophy.
No poetry.
[Educati]
Professional Studies.
Education to produce engineers or bankers.
Positivism in Belgium (France again!).
Hannon.
Altmeyer, that old Bag!
His description.
His style.

General hatred of literature.

134. BRUSSELS
BELGIAN SPIRIT

[hatred]

No Latin. No Greek. Professional studies. Make bankers. Hatred of poetry. A Latinist would make a bad businessman.

Lord Duruy wants to make France another Belgium.

Latin studies. As far as possible, no poets, or very few poets. — No metaphysics. No philosophy class.

Positivism in Belgium.

Altmeyer and Hannon.

Hatred of Belgium for all literature, & especially for La Bruyère.

---

135. 15. THE FRENCH LANGUAGE IN BELGIUM

— Style of the few books written here.

— Some samples of Belgian vocabulary.

— Nobody knows French, but it is customary to pretend not knowing Flemish. The proof that they know it very well is that they *harangue* their servants in Flemish.

> It does not taste me.
> I don't like that — I does.
> Inflate.
> I can't sleep.
> Are you coming with?
> Etc. Etc.

136. BRUSSELS
GENERAL CHARACTERISTICS
POLITICS

> I maintain Proppining up.[25]
> (Verhaegen)[26]
> \< Founder of a University for *Free Thinking*. \>

137. BRUSSELS
GENERAL CHARACTERISTICS
CUSTOMS

Before the Kaulbach made in the style of *Werther*, two Belgians. One says to the other: That's mythology, isn't it?[27]

Everything they don't understand is categorized as mythology.

There's plenty.

138. LITTLE ODDITIES

Belgian style.
Mr. Reyer is almost finished.

139. ODDITIES

Two Englishmen take me for Mr. Wiertz.[28]

The painted parrot of the *Montagne-aux-Herbes-Potagères*.

Milady, if you make a move, you ......

140. BRUSSELS ODDITIES

In the Rue *Nuit et Jour*, at a neighborhood fair, a vacillation:

— Dear Madame, says Athos, if you *move* [resistance] a finger, *I'll* blow your brains out.

— *Dear Sir, you're* going to go straight to .....

141. ODDITIES

Amusing correspondence of the *Office of Publicity*.
<Ask Arthur.>

Specimens of the Belgian style, to be found in the catalog of perfumeries.

Pro refrigerio animæ suæ.[29]
Translated by Mr. Wauters.

Odd Latin of the inscriptions.

Garden of zoology, horticulture, and *amenity*.

The tomb of David (where?).
Since they came to look for the remains of a barely known Cavaignac, they could have thought of David, who was illustrious *&* exiled too.[30]

142. BRUSSELS
HEALTH. DISEASES

Ophthalmia, which the Belgians generally call *hospitalmia*.

143. BRUSSELS
    BELGIAN STYLE

The Grelot says in regard to Napoléon III: "He is said to be very ill. It's of little importance. He will die *of what he must die*"— from that which must kill him.

Besides, when it is said here that the Emperor is well, one passes for a spy. It is customary, among *people of good company*, to say that he is very ill.

Belgian conformity.
Belgian obedience.
Belgian sheepery.

The friends of Proudhon during the riot. Figures of speech.

144. BRUSSELS
    CUSTOMS

Lord Altmeyer.
"That, I admire."
[Phob of priests]
Priest-o-phobia.
Curses. *Free thinker*; it says everything.
The daughter of Altmeyer: "I stuck Proudhon."
Mad. de Stael *&* the German professor.
<u>Sues</u> *eum non cognoverunt.*[31]

145–146. BRUSSELS

Belgian Expressions

Confidential diseases.

[I have] <My soul has> thought a lot about this Belgian word.

Confidential seems absurd to me; because, although it's true that such diseases are transmitted only in secrecy and privacy, it's quite certain that, among the French <at least>, one doesn't announce in advance, even when one knows it, <one-self>,> *the confidence* in question to the person to whom it is *desired* to transmit it.

Joy and triumph! *Eureka*! This word probably derives from the excessively prudish, stupid, & delicate character of this subtle Belgian people! — Thus I suppose that in Brussels high society, a girl does not say:

— *That young man fucked me the pox.*

— And that young man does not say, in speaking of a well-bred girl: *She gave me the gift that keeps on giving!*

They would rather say, the first person: — *That young man shared a very nasty confidence with me!* [and the other] or rather: *That young man gave me such a horrible confidence that my hair fell out!* and the other:

She has given me a confidence which I shall remember for a long time! or: *I have given her my confidence! Her offspring will remember it until the third generation!*

O Good Belgian pharmacists! I *passionately* love your dictionary, and Euphemism dominates, in [your eloquence] your advertisements!

147. BRUSSELS
CUSTOMS

Belgian Expressions

Find a little book used by the Belgians, enumerating the:

Do not say …… but say ……

It doesn't taste me.

Do you taste that?

Do you know how to?

If ya like? (more abbreviated than the vaudevillisme)

For once.

Do action (history of the gravedigger).

Confidential diseases.

The wandering of dogs.
(*Hydrophobia (rabies)*).
Hopitalmie.

Knowing how [savoir] instead of being able [pouvoir].

When are you leaving? — I cannot leave. — Why? — I don't have any money.

I can't sleep.

I can't eat anymore.

148. BRUSSELS

Belgian Expressions

The ministry has just did an act that ......

This ministry, [in the five years] since it opened, has not yet done a single act.

A gravedigger had [opened a] *dug up* a coffin, *broke* it open, *raped* the corpse (as much as an inert being can be raped), and *stole* the jewelry buried with the dead. — The lawyer of the gravedigger: "I will show that my client did not *do* any of the things that he is accused of."

Ah! Victor Joly is quite right in advising them to forget French and to reacquaint themselves with Flemish. But unfortunately V. Joly is obliged to write that in French.

149. Belgian Expressions

[Press clipping from *Gand* (July 8, 1864) in which a solicitor is questioned about his political opinions. In the interview, the solicitor is forced to classify himself by choosing what political camp he belongs to. CB focuses on the phrase "*Je n'avais posé aucun acte…*"]

150. Belgian Expressions

[Press clipping containing a list of expressions overheard in the street.]

151. 16. JOURNALISTS AND LITTERATEURS

In general, the litterateur (?) has another job. — Office worker, — most often.

For the rest, there is no literature. Two or three singers, Flemish monkeys of Beranger's mischievousness.[32]

Scientists, annalists, [that is to say] that means, people who buy a stack of papers at a low price [repr] (accounts [of archi] of fees) [,] for buildings and for other things, communal council meeting records, archival copies, etc.) and then sell the whole thing as a history book — strictly speaking, everyone here is an *annalist*, or a dealer of paintings *&* oddities.

The tone of journalism. Many examples.
< Ridiculous correspondence of the *Office of Publicity.* >
L'Indépendance belge.
L'Écho du parlement.
L'Étoile belge.
Le Journal de Bruxelles.
Le Bien Public.
Le Sancho.
Le Grelot.
L'Espiègle.
Etc., etc., etc.

Literary patriotism. A poster for a show.

152. BRUSSELS
GENERAL CHARACTERISTICS
CUSTOMS

No journalism.
They don't believe the journalist.
What journalism!

Here you can print that God is a rascal, but if you printed that Belgium isn't perfect, you would be stoned.
The modesty of *L'Espiègle*, relative to girls.

Here one can cheat in business. But give your arm to your mistress, you are dishonored.

About modesty, the trial of Mr. Keym.

153. BRUSSELS
POLITICS
RELIGION

All of Belgium is left to the infamous *Siècle*, which is only ridiculous in France, but which, among barbarous people, like this one, is a loathsome journal.

154. Flemish coarseness

Graciousness amongst colleagues

[Press clipping from the journal *la Paix* about a dialogue between Catholic newspapers, which contains a response to the line: "So many cocks on the same manure pile will have a hard time living there …" "Manure! the word is hard for the readers of clerical papers."]

155. [Press clipping from *Indépendance belge* (January 20, 1865) about the death of Proudhon. His book, *Property is Theft*, is referred to as Aristophanic vaudeville. Proudhon, who sought to dissolve society, is mocked for seeking the consolation of his family in his final

days. In the margins, CB writes: *Remarkable tact of the corresponding French writers from* L'Indépendance *about the death of Proudhon. Perhaps the article is by a vaudevilliste who is advertising himself. He loved his family, this monster! Like Catilina, who surprised Mérimée so much.*]

156. [Press clipping from *L'Espiègle* (Vol. 12, N⁰ 8) titled "A Touching Story." This article concerns a publishing house that printed more copies of an author's work than permitted and an honest employee's denunciation of the theft. The company seems to have taken revenge against its accuser. In the margins, CB writes: *Possible charges in Belgium. There are signs in the street, thanks to Belgian liberty, announcing that Mr. X ... is a cuckold. No complaints, no revenge, no lawsuit. What should we think of the accuser, and of the accused, who bears the accusation?*]

157. POOR BELGIUM
    JOURNALISM

"The Grand Duke heir of Russia died in Nice. It is said that the Emperor loved his son very much. It is permissible to doubt the paternal love of certain Sires." — *Espiègle*, political weekly.

I suppose that the quip turns on the word: Sire, a Fine example of a democratic Belgian spirit.

(*Browse all the newspaper issues that I have collected, and extract the articles for which I kept them.*)

158. BRUSSELS
Literary Customs

See the December 25, 1864 issue of *L'Espiègle*. (Blackmail. — Comparing the romantic inscriptions in Belgian latrines to the romantic correspondence of the *Office of Publicity*.)

CONCLUSION FOR BRUSSELS

.... In brief, Brussels is what we call a *Hole*, but not a harmless hole.

A Hole full of scandalmongers. A new hat.

---

159. BELGIUM
    CUSTOMS

> Correspondence of the *Office of Publicity*:
> *Nursery of Saint-Josse-Ten-Noode.*

"A wish was granted to two loves: to the achievement of this ardently awaited craving, the promise has been sworn on Heaven to give FIVE FRANCS to the *little angels* of the nursery.

Receive, Monsieur Bertram, this *simple offering*, *&* make, if it pleases you, *your golden-haired cherubs* pray for the happiness of the two souls who have sworn before *God* (the God of the Belgians?) to share unswerving love for each other *&* [feli] faithfulness. S.M."

The idyll among the Brutes.
Gessner among the Brutes.
The idealism of the Brutes.
(Look for lots of correspondence samples in *The Office.*)

161. BRUSSELS. CUSTOMS
    BELGIAN JOURNALISM
    L'ESPIÈGLE

THE MINISTRY'S VOICE

A representative of the Left, famous for his witticisms, is already planning for the moment when he alone will make up the majority of the ministry.

It is, indeed, to be foreseen, in the state of loss and sc..w-ups where the left [is] stands. Then the Lapalisse in question will say with pride: "I am the voice [of the Ministry] of the majority; salutations!" And in order not to lose his voice, he will go to Arlon; [he will go to Arlon]; he will go to bed like a woman in labor; a carriage will permanently remain at his doorstep, for serious cases. They'll make him laugh, and amuse him in every way, to keep him in good condition. The little H. will tickle his behind, and the anticlerical Monsieur Defré will chant the vespers, with his contrite air, and the happy *&* faithful servant to the ministry will exclaim, "You can take my backside away, if it will make them happier!"

162. BRUSSELS
BELGIAN JOURNALISM

A vigorous man. A barbarian, moreover — Mr. Victor Joly, who accepts, without believing, the *two-part* epistles of Victor Hugo.

V. Joly, like those [real] lovers, despises what he loves, and loves what he despises. V. Joly is a patriot. Rare merit in a country *where* there is no homeland.

!!!

A Belgian moves forward, not with rhythm, but with all *congenital heaviness*.

163. THE FINE ARTS AND EXAMPLES OF THE
 DELICATESSE OF BELGIAN CRITICISM

[Press clipping from *Sancho* (Sept. 25, 1864) ridiculing Corot, Delacroix, and Diaz for paintings that are not realistic. Excerpts: "Were their paintings not actually destined for some exhibition in New South Wales or Tombouctou? Are they perhaps traps for our naïve Flemish credulity? Is the curator of the exhibition quite certain that the painting of Courbet, representing two *Gougnottes* — initiates will understand this word, invented for the needs of the thing, in some *lupanar* of a lower floor — was intended for a public exhibition?"] [33]

| 164. BRUSSELS
Theaters,
pleasures,
customs. | Always great care taken to advise the public when the author is Belgian, *rara avis*. [34] |

RE-OPENING OF THE NATIONAL CIRCUS
THEATER

by a French troupe (SUMMER SEASON)

Rue du Cirque

JUNE 10, SATURDAY. FIRST REPRESENTATION OF
THE MAN
WITH THE
BLACK MASK

Great historical & ORIGINAL drama in 5 acts and 10 tableaux, a great spectacle, with choruses of 40 people.
by Alexandre Dandoé
(YOUNG BELGIAN AUTHOR)

The orchestra & choirs will be directed by M.J.B. Braun (the poster of the day will give the details of the show).

NOTICE. — The management is sure that <u>the whole of Brussels</u> will come to see and hear the work of this young metal-founder; that everyone will bring his tribute of encouragement to this bold <u>Brusselian author</u> who offers up to public criticism his first lines through a moving drama, whose energetic scenes, the hearty text, will leave in the opinion of his <u>countrymen</u> a <u>profound satisfaction</u> and a <u>legitimate pride</u> !!! [35]

165. 17. BELGIAN IMPIETY

>Insults to the Pope.
>Propaganda of impiety.
>Death of the Archbishop of Paris.
>Performance of the *Jesuit* play.[36]
>The Jesuit — Puppet.
>A procession.
>Royal Subscription for funerals.
>Against a Catholic teacher.
>About the cemetery law.
>Lay burials.
>Contested or stolen corpses.
>A Solidarist funeral.
>Lay burial of a woman.
>
>Analysis of the Rules of the *Libre Pensée*.
>Testamentary formula.
>
>The wager of two host eaters.

166. *Belgian crudity and impiety*

>The sole Gaulois in Belgium.
>Excrement everywhere.
>Dogs, pissers, vomitters.
>
>THE WAGER OF THE HOST EATERS.

167. News at hand
 [Press clipping from *L'Espiègle* (January 1865) about a holy brother who is mocked for his disparities (a big man who cries, stubborn but tolerant, greedy but generous, despotic but liberal, etc.). CB reacts to the final statement about him being an amiable old man, vulgarly referred to as Pope IX, saying: *The playful and mischievous tone vis-à-vis the pope. The greatest Belgian joke, the most refined, with regard to the pope, is to call him* pio nono. *And to say the name of the pope in Italian is for the flock of Belgian monkeys the infallible means of rendering him ridiculous.*]

168. [Press clippings from *Le Grelot* (January 1865) about the death of Pope IX, who is referred to as the Old Carp. The second clipping is this passage in Latin & French: *Quos vult perdere Jupiter dementat, et Pio déménage.*] [37]

169. Unholy Societies
 [Press clipping from *L'Espiègle* (Feb. 1865), which CB says "welcomes the rapidity of Belgian *progress*." The article is about two journals and how their denunciations of atheism only serve to increase the number of atheists. It also notes how one society of atheists does not admit any form of worship whereas others admit

Deists. Germany, Switzerland, Spain, France, America, and England are already represented, Baudelaire notes, "by the names of their greatest thinkers."]

170. (*L'Espiègle* recounts the death of the Archbishop of Paris)
[Press clipping about a priest arguing with insurgents that death by slow resignation is superior to death by gunshot. As a general is heard screaming for the people to come kill him, the priest blissfully says to him, "Surrender and take back your chains, for if you die in the street, your remains, like those of a dog, would not bring me anything." In the margins, CB writes: *Sample of Belgian style, Belgian delicacy, Belgian elevation, etc. Priest-o-phobia.*]

171. Jesuit Phobia
Le Jésuite
[Press clipping from *L'Entracte* (August 18, 1864) about a play called *The Jesuit* and the audience's response to it. The applause went to the actor playing the Jesuit, not to the "vile machinations of a man whose sight alone revolts all generous feelings." CB's comment: *Jesuit phobia.*]

172. Jesuit Phobia

[Press clipping from *La Paix* (July 31, 1864) about an analogy between Pir Jan Klaes, a red-nosed hunchback puppet, and the Jesuit. The puppeteer brings Klaes on stage once an audience grows bored with the main show. When the crowd abandons the theater, the directors abandon the old repertory and wield with a terrible hand the model-Jesuit, this ugly braggart that will capture all the liberal inheritances if the Dechamps program is accepted by the Crown and the country.[38] The audience is moved by this sight and the *liards* rain down. "Without the devil, the prank of Pir Jan Klaes is impossible; — without the Jesuit, the government party would not reign for six months."]

173- BELGIAN IMPIETY

174. [Press clipping from *Le Grelot. Charivari belge.* Tirage 282 397 (Thursday, Sept. 15, 1864). A report describing a religious procession: "I can never look at a procession without laughing and without taking pity on humanity." CB's focus is on the style of the prose. His sole comment: *Belgian style.*]

175- Rationalist newspaper. Sold at F. Claassen's, 2 rue
176. Cantersteen Street.
[Press clipping from *Le Libre Examen* (Dec. 10, 1864) about the anger of Freethinkers over the King dispensing monies to a religious association when the civil authority is secular.]

177. [Press clipping from *Libre examen* (June 1, 1864), the main part of which addresses a Catholic teacher who denounces a young girl, saying that she is lost if she no longer carries a rosary, and that if she does not have ultra-Catholic ideas, she is weakened by "the breath of desire." In the margin, CB writes: *Letter from a subscriber against a Catholic teacher. Always the affirmation that nothing is better than natural life.*]

178. [Press clipping from *Sancho* (Sept. 25, 1864) about cemetery laws and the desire of free thinkers and philosophers to be buried amongst Catholics. In the margin, CB simply writes: *Important article.*]

179. [Brochure outlining the statutes of *La Libre Pensée*, the association for the organization of civil funerals, which was founded in Brussels on January 19, 1863.]

180. [Copy of *La Libre Pensée*'s last will and testament.]

181. [Copy of a statute from *La Libre Pensée*'s last will & testament.]

182. [Invitation to the General Assembly of *La Libre Pensée*, November 28, 1864.]

183. [Press clippings from *Libre examen* (June 10, 1864) about education as discussed by the Antwerp subcommittee of Free Thought, civil burials, the bad faith of certain journals for reporting the burial ceremony, the lack of respect for freedom of opinion, etc. The concluding remark is about convincing people of the eminently domineering and mercantile nature of all religions. The reporter concludes: "We believe that this day will not be lost for the cause of free examination."[39] CB writes in the margins: *Once again! What a triumph!*]

184. SOLIDARISTS
 Burials
 Disputed corpses
 (The corpse of Patroclus.)
 [Press clipping from the *Tribune du peuple* (Nov. 10, 1865) about attacks against Solidarists and the actions of certain priests (the manipulation of people

on their deathbeds), which the newspaper denounces.
It concludes with a Baron's protest: "Am I not a free
thinker, an avowed enemy of all villainy, dissimulation, subterfuge, in a word, all the lies of virtuous
Catholics?"]

185. Solidarists
Burials
Belgian impiety

[Lengthy June 5, 1864 press clipping about the burial
of a Solidarist and the manifestations of their impiety, including the refusal of religious intercession.
"Whenever we pay final homage to the heroic death
of one of our own and when we return to the earth,
our common mother, the remains of a free thinker, a
true man; every time then, from this pit where the
memories of so much grandeur and so much misery are buried, a cry of supreme insurrection rises, a
cry of victory & intellectual revolt AGAINST GOD,
AGAINST THE SKY AND EARTH, against iniquity,
injustice, & the reign of force. The Church trembles
in its foundations & souls feel stirred. [...] He saw,
one by one, his chamber brothers, succumbing to
most sicknesses as perfect Catholics; but he, while
sharing their sorrows, knew how to dominate by his
moral vigor this distressing spectacle of weaknesses

and corruption, to repudiate the priest, to die as a free man, and finally to prove that PEACE OF SOUL IS IN THE NEGATION OF GOD!]

186. CIVIL BURIAL OF A WOMAN

[Lengthy press clipping from *Libre examen* (June 1, 1864) about the burial of Jeanne Deleener, an intelligent and firm woman who refused the local priest until her final hour, in spite of all the clerical man's numerous and intrusive acts. The bright shining of the torch of reason is celebrated for resisting Catholicism's claim to "its things," the soul and intelligence. Deleener's death is praised as a last protest against false gods and she for her refusal to become the client, prey, and toy of a church enemy.]

186A. BRUSSELS CHURCHES

Closed churches.
What becomes of the money collected from tourists?
Catholicism in Belgium resembles both Neapolitan Superstition & Protestant Priggery.

———

A procession. Finally! Banners on a rope, crossing the street. A phrase of Delacroix's on the flags.

The processions in France, suppressed for the sake of some murderers *&* heretics. Do you remember the incense, the shower of roses, etc. ... ?

Byzantine banners, so heavy that some of them were carried flat.

Devout bourgeois. Those types are just as stupid as the revolutionaries.

187. 18. PRIEST-O-PHOBIA
IRRELIGION

>   Again *Libre Pensée*.
>   Again the *Solidaires* and the *Affranchis*.[40]
>   Another *testamentary formula*:
>   to steal the corpse from the church.
>   An article by Mr. Sauvestre on *Libre Pensée*.[41]
>   Again the *stolen corpses*.
>   Funeral of an abbot who died as a *free thinker*.
>   Jesuit phobia.

> > What it is about *our brave De Buck*, an ex-convict, persecuted by the Jesuits.[42]

An assembly of *Libre Pensée*, at my hotel, at the *Grand Miroir*. Belgian philosophical remarks.

Another Solidaire funeral, to the tune of: *Damn! so! if your sister is sick!*

— The clerical party and the liberal party.
— I suspect them to be equally stupid.

The famous Defré (the Belgian version of Paul-Louis Courier) is afraid of ghosts, digs up the corpses of the ungodly to put them in holy ground, believes that he will die like Courier, and is accompanied at night so as not to be assassinated by the Jesuits.[43] — My first interview with this imbecile. He was drunk — he had interrupted the music to make a speech about progress & against Rubens as a Catholic painter.

Abolishers of the death penalty, — very interested without a doubt.

— Belgian impiety is a counterfeit of French impiety cubed.

< Opinion of a Companion of Dumouriez about Belgian political parties. >

Ugliness & debauchery of the Flemish clergy. —

The dogs' or outcasts' corner. *The Funeral* [of] < by > [Félicien] Rops.

Belgian bigotry. — Anthropophagous Christians in South America. — A program by Mr. de Caston.[44]

188. BRUSSELS
GENERAL CHARACTERISTICS

Belgium is more full than any other country with people who believe that J.C. was *a great man*, that *nature* [teac] teaches nothing but good, that *universal morality* has preceded dogmas in all religions, that *man can do everything*, even create a language, and that steam, railways, & gas lighting prove the *eternal* progress of mankind.

All these old leftovers [of the [French philosophism] <of a philosophy of exportation> are swallowed here like [heavenly] <sublime> sweets. In short, what Belgium, always apelike, imitates with the greatest happiness and *naturalness*, is French stupidity.

(The Memphite stone
in relation to progress.)[45]

189. [Press clipping from the *Société des Libres Penseurs* bearing the epigraph: "More priests at birth, marriage, & death." The article concerns the refusal of last rites and the evocation of the motto of the Free Thinkers: *Peace of soul is born of the negation of God.* A distinction is made between the Free Thinkers & the Solidarists, who are deists. The article concludes by stating that Catholic journals have no need to be indignant since such societies are created only to resist the invasions of the clergy.]

190. [Double of 180]

191. BRUSSELS
Priest-o-Phobia

Delicacy of Belgian style.
Wild jackal and Catholic priest.

"In Zoology there are two individuals on whom the corpse exercises a unique influence: the jackal and the Catholic priest. As soon as death has enveloped, or is about to envelop a human creature with its shroud, you see them both obeying their instincts, smelling the wind, picking up the scent, and rushing to the body with frightening shamelessness, while thinking to themselves: There's something to be done."
— LE GRELOT (February 16, 1865)

Much later *Le Grelot* accuses the priest of stealing corpses. Take note that the freethinker, too, thinks about nothing but stealing corpses. Both the priest & the freethinker play tug of war with corpses, resulting in their being dismembered.

Le Grelot always refers to *Pio nono* in a casual manner. *Pio nono* derobes; which means: the Pope is deranged.

192. Brussels

> November 15, 1864

> THE FREE THOUGHT
> ASSOCIATION
> FOR
> THE MIND'S EMANCIPATION
> THROUGH THE INSTRUCTION
> AND
> ORGANIZATION OF CIVIL
> BURIALS
>
> N° 37

> Mr. —

The Governing Board invites you to attend
the funeral of Mr.

> Abbey Louis Joseph Dupont,
>
> formerly serving the diocese of Tournai,

died a free thinker in Brussels, on this night, after a long illness, at 63 years of age.

The funeral will take place Thursday, the 17th of this month, at 3 o'clock, in the town cemetery, near Hall gate.

> We will meet, at 2:30,

at the house of the deceased, 44 Rue Blaes.

> The Secretary   The President
> Paul Ithier   Henri Bergé

193. POLITICS
PRIEST-O-PHOBIA

A very brief account of the affair of *our brave* De Buck. Songs and caricatures against the Jesuits.

194. POLITICS
PRIEST-O-PHOBIA

An assembly of *Libre Pensée* at my hotel.

Different speeches.

A fanatic complains that the *free thinkers* are still so weak as to allow the contagion to enter the building.

It's not enough to be a *free thinker* for oneself. Your wife must not go to mass or confession.

Telemachus, Calypso, Jesus Christ, etc., etc., etc., etc. ...... and other mythologies. Everything is in the moral *&* [in] in feeling.

The very hot weather makes me take off my clothes, O Mary mother of God! The very cold weather that made me put them back on, O Mary mother of God!

The Ursulines were given land. They will poison your children.[46]

Civil funeral of Armellini.[47]

"The multitude of freethinkers followed."

A people should be considered lucky if they have a multitude of such men!

We others, we have only one per century.

194. CUSTOMS. PRIEST-O-PHOBIA

Did you know that a corpse was stolen?
Did he want to eat it?

The pleasure of seeing a very ridiculous politician. Had he been French, I would have taken the same pleasure.

Mr. Defré, a radical. *Useful art*. Rubens should have supported Protestantism with his brush.

In short, French socialism, turned hideous. It's the Elephant, imitating the fandango, or the egg dance.[48]

Fouriérism.

Alas! he was drunk, a Representative!

Persecutor of M.-J. Proudhon, in a free country.

196- POLITICS
196a. PRIEST-O-PHOBIA

The clerical party and the revolutionary party. Each can reproach the other for something.
But what violence!
What the Revolutionaries are. Example: Defré.
They believe in every stupid thing the French Liberals put forth.

(Abolition of the Death penalty. Victor Hugo dominates like Courbet. [I learn] <I'm told> that 30,000 people in Paris petition for the abolition of the death penalty, 30,000 people who deserve it. If you shudder, then you are already guilty. Or, in any case, you're directly implicated in the question. The excessive love of life is a descent into animality.) In France atheism is polite. Here, it is violent, stupid, emphatic. Belgian stupidity is an enormous counterfeit of French stupidity — it is French stupidity cubed.

Trois Sociétés, whose aim is to persuade, & even to compel the citizens to die like dogs. What is the dog corner. The funniest thing is that these *"future dogs"* want to be buried with Christians.

The *free thinker* (thinka, as Belgians say) of the high classes, that is to say the rich brutes, owns a newspaper: *Le Libre Examen*, a *rationalist newspaper*.

Here are a few quotes:

....

[you] you see what a rationalist is.

The other two Societies (for lower classes) are the *Affranchis & * the *Solidaires*. Funerals with music. Brass. Trombones.

Civil burial passing through Place de la Monnaie. Corpses at the doorstep of the estaminets.[49]

Stolen corpses. ("They gone took a body!") Did they want to eat it!

Danger of associating with any group. Abdication of the individual.

197. POLITICS
PRIEST-O-PHOBIA

And they come back drunk, blowing in their trombones: *Ah! damn! then if your sister is sick!*[50] purposely pass by a church, devised an itinerary to disturb a presbytery, very proud to have thrown a solidarist into the void. *Those who do not believe in the immortality of their being do themselves justice,* — said Robespierre.

Quotation of the Rules *&* formulas of the will of free thinkers.

It is said that Pelletan is part of the thing.[51]

Some speeches on the graves of *solidarists* and *free thinkers*.

198. DIGNITY OF THE BELGIAN CLERGY

Preaching against drunkenness by a drunken Redemptorist. Successive *peripeteia*.

199. POLITICS
PRIEST-O-PHOBIA

The question of cemeteries & burials.
[Moreover]
Brutalities of the clergy. The dogs' corner, the reprobates. The corpse thrown over the wall.

Incidentally, *The Burial* (by Rops) (the story of the priest reproaching Cadart)[52] demonstrates the vulgarity of the Belgian clergy. This clergy is vulgar because it is Belgian, not because it is Roman.

Even I was shocked by this:
It is forbidden to visit churches at any time; it is forbidden to walk in them; it is forbidden to pray in them except during the service hours.

After all, why shouldn't the clergy [also] be as vulgar as the rest of the nation? Like prostitutes who don't practice gallantry, as certain priests don't practice religion.

200. BRUSSELS
   GENERAL TRAITS

The Belgians remind me of the Christian cannibals [of the America of the South] of South America. One finds among them, hanging from the trees, Christian emblems whose meaning is unknown to them.

At what rung of the human species, or of the simian species, would the Belgian belong to?

The Christian idea (the invisible God: creator, omniscient, conscious, omnipresent) cannot enter a Belgian brain.

Here there are only atheists or superstitious people.

---

201. [Program of Alfred de Caston]

202. BRUSSELS
   POLITICAL CUSTOMS

The Congress of Malines.[53]

Too many censors. Too many compliments. The Flemish vice, the love of rank, the love of chattering, is found among Catholics.

Hermann
Dupanloup
Félix
De Kerchove
Janmot
Van Schendel

For Belgians Commissions are an excuse to gain rank, just as triumphal arches are a reason to throw parties.

203. 19. POLITICS

    Electoral customs.

                             < The cost of the election
    Electoral scandals.   according to locality. >

    Parliamentary politeness.

    Ridiculous discussion about electoral measures.

    Republican meeting.
           < Counterfeiting Jacobinism.
             Belgium always late,
            a century in arrears.

204. BRUSSELS
POLITICAL CUSTOMS

(Nothing is more ridiculous than to seek truth in numbers.)

Universal Suffrage and table turning.[54] It's man seeking *truth* in man. (!!!) Voting is therefore only a means of creating *a policy* — it is mechanical, in despair of reason, *a desideratum*.

205. BRUSSELS
POLITICAL CUSTOMS

The Elections.
The flocks of Electors.
The meetings (Lacroix, various picturesque scenes).
The beautiful *orators*.
The caricatures.
The price of an election!

A keepsake of all the songs *&* caricatures against the Jesuits.

206. BRUSSELS
POLITICAL CUSTOMS

Mr. Vleminckx, go wash yourself![55] Five *centimes*.
Electors, have pity on the poor blind. (Copy the poster.)
Everyone. *I said!*
Caricature contra the liberals.
Caricature contra the clerics.
One right next to the other.

They had agreed, according to a correspondence from Charleroi, not to insult Mr. Deschamps.

Magnanimous people!

A corpse of people. A talkative corpse, created by diplomacy.

The French have praised America and Belgium quite a lot. I bet at this very moment, about the elections....

207. [Proo]
BRUSSELS
POLITICS

"According to the parliamentary documents, the draft of the bill intended to punish acts of fraud in electoral matters."

Follow the draft bill below.
$$\text{37 articles!!!!}$$
To avoid EVERY KIND of SAVAGERY!
Three full columns in *L'Indépendance Belge.*

Besides, it's a well-known fact in Belgium that such an election, in such a locality, costs so much. The price is known, for [all] all localities (trial for election expenses).

---

208. **BRUSSELS**
POLITICAL CUSTOMS

Mr. Uleminckx, go wash yourself!
Five *centimes.*
Belgian spirit: delicate, fine, polite, subtle, ingenious.

209. ELECTORAL CUSTOMS

[Press clipping from *Écho de Bruxelles* (August 5, 1864) about organized bands of armed Catholics (The Society of St. Joseph) making illegal demonstrations. *Stad Gent*, a liberal Flemish journal from Ghent, denounces the Josephites, stating that they were bribed and enlisted to act on others' orders.]

210. Elections
Restricted suffrage
Universal suffrage
[Press clipping from *La Paix* (July 31, 1864) about the contradictory attitudes of the French newspaper *Le Siècle*. When not in power, it protests against governmental intervention in electoral battles. Contrarily, it claims to enlighten voters and is audacious enough to advise the Belgian cabinet not to surrender votes to clerical actions without fighting. Doctrinaire Belgians blame the intervention of the French government on the elections, but struggle with the extent of its influence. The *palinodie* is scandalous. This government intervention is especially dangerous under the restricted suffrage regime. Universal suffrage makes it less formidable: thousands of citizens cannot be bribed.]

211. Vow to go see if the little old woman is at the edge of the canal.

POOR BELGIUM

About cheap life, the only cheap thing is a *seat* in the House. An election here is not so expensive. Some deputies haven't paid more than 30,000 francs for theirs. It's cheap compared to England and the United States. This proves that a Belgian conscience is not expensive <, and that the Belgian palace is not refined >.

The quip of Mr. Coomans.[56] (On ELECTORAL *matters*).

I have lost the price chart of the Elections, drawn up [by] according to localities.

212. [Press clipping from *Sancho* (August 21, 1864) about scandalous aspects of the previous election. In Bastogne, the liberals are stoned; in Ghent, the Catholics are shaken up. Arithmetic becomes an inexact science adapted to the needs of the cause. If the House honors the country, it will vote on the electoral fraud act.]

213. Belgium
Political customs

See the discussions on electoral reform in the *Journal de Liège* (corridors, partitions).

Friday July 28, 1865
Écho du Parlement

Mr. Tesch (Minister): The voter doesn't owe an explanation to anyone .... The voter exercises his sovereign right ... It's a right he exercises *&* not a duty he fulfills.

Mr. Coomans (opposition): It's the voters' feudalism.

Mr. Tesch: You say nothing but hot air, as usual.

Mr. de Borchgrave (Ministerial): [I have not] I did not hear, but if I had heard, I would answer back, eh! (Laughter)

(About election expenses, election allowances, miscellaneous, transportation, etc.)

214. PARLIAMENTARY POLITENESS

[Press clipping from *L'Espiègle* (January 31, 1865) summarizing the previous legislative year and documenting accusations of corruption, venality, insults, abused expedition laws, and a senator accusing the Minister of Finance with corruption.]

215. Parliamentary Amenities

216. QUESTIONS ON ANTWERP

[Lengthy press clipping from *Indépendance belge* (November 27, 1864) comprised of a fractious discussion between the Minister for Foreign Affairs & others from the Antwerp Chamber of Commerce. The piece abounds with insults and accusations revolving around Antwerp's prosperity, or lack thereof, and the obstacles in its path.]

217. Parliamentary Amenities

[Lengthy press clipping from *Étoile Belge* (June 3, 1864) of another fractious discussion between politicians, this time about cemeteries and an allegedly falsified circular. It devolves into insults, accusations, and interpositions, with demands for a call to order to be maintained by the president.]

218. Parliamentary Amenities

[Press clipping from *Étoile Belge* (June 3, 1864) involving a discussion between the president of the assembly and several other politicians, including someone described as an ardent, fiery orator, overflowing with indignation, an orator who is the hope of the old Roman party. The main topic concerns the insulting of Bara, who is called a buffoon.]

219. Ridiculous discussion about electoral measures
[Extremely lengthy press clipping from *Journal de Liége* (July 24, 1865). A vote is mocked as an "alphabetic disorder" while voters are said to require being educated before a new vote can occur. In opposition, someone calls for the elimination of the election, as that would be more honest. Voter secrecy is questioned, as the possible amendment of a law, and questions of fraud and electoral corruption are broached.]

220. Electoral Measures
[Press clipping from *Journal de Liége* (July 24, 1865) about resolutions taken to protect voters from the control of the clergy, especially in the Flemish countryside. Also discussed here is developing voter secrecy through the use of corridors and partitions, with questions being raised about how to handle blind and disabled voters.]

221. Electoral Measures
[Press clipping titled "The Puppets of the Day" (August 1, 1864) mocking the devices designed to protect voter secrecy. The voter booth is referred to as a strange cloakroom and theater from which, in the name of modesty, young girls & adolescents should be removed.]

222. [Continuation of section 219]

223. [Lengthy press clipping from *La Rive Gauche* (Sunday, Nov. 5, 1865) reporting on a Republican meeting that brought together the Brussels Socialist Democrats and French students returning from the Congress of Liege and leaving to relocate under the odious yoke that weighs on unfortunate France. Part of the material concerns the trial of the Belgian press, which altered speeches made in congress. Only two newspapers (*la Gazette de Liège* and *l'Echo de Liège*) are said to have shown good faith for revealing the odious, anti-social consequences of Catholicism. The speeches are infused with aggressive violence. CB underlined many passages. Here are some: Citizen Tridon, a French student, notes that the struggle is between Man and God, between the future and the past, and that Rome, the palace of the Popes, is the center of action and must be attacked and destroyed. Catholicism he says is the great adversary of the Revolution and the Revolution must annihilate it through force. Citizen Casse says, let us be distinct, straightforward, and boldly revolutionary or return to Rome and kiss the Pope's mule. Citizen Sibrac speaks of the cordial and fraternal assembly and thanks women for coming, stating that we need to know with them why we fight, then noting that they must not remain outside

the Revolutionary movement, they must follow us in every effort of social renovation. They will not fail us, I am sure. It was Eve who uttered the first cry of revolt against God. Citizen Brismée denounces the bourgeois as murderers and thieves while another citizen proclaims that students are the Vanguard of Progress, for they have knowledge. Men must unite he says in the great principle of mutuality and reject any extramural idea that has no foundation. War on God! — progress is there. Citizen César de Paepe speaks of there being positivists, atheists, and revolutionaries in Belgium and that all of them want social reform. Citizen Rey says freedom will reign soon; the slaves will become the masters — there is room for everyone in the great sun of the Revolution. Another calls out, To arms! Citizen Jacquelard argues that revealing oppression is not sufficient; the bourgeoisie must be defeated. Our congress will be different from that of the one in Liege. Ours will stand in the street, and our rifles will conclude. Citizens, to instruct the people, it is useless to speak to them of Taine, Comte, and Littré. They feel their misery and want to escape. That is enough! Citizen Pellerin: Men are brothers, we must support the disabled as well as the abled. We talked of the guillotine; we only want to reverse the obstacles. If a hundred thousand heads obstruct us, let them fall, yes; but we only have love for the human community... etc. The editor of the article concludes: After what we have read, we will understand that our role is reduced to little. What could we say now that did not seem cold? This evening was truly wonderful; it is the most energetic, the most fraternal, the broadest, the most beautiful thing we have ever heard of the Social Revolution. The orators, acclaimed and supported by unanimous and frenetic bravos, succeeded each other in the tribune as if carried away by the irresistible torrent of the Idea. At every moment it seemed to us to feel the genius of the Revolution pass over the assembly and purify it of its fire. *Angelo.*]

224. 20. POLITICS

There is no such thing as the "Belgian people." There are hostile races and hostile cities. Take Antwerp, for example. Belgium, a diplomatic [harle] harlequin.

— Baroque history of the Brabant Revolution, carried out against a philosopher King, and facing the French Revolution, a philosophical revolution.

— A constitutional King is an automaton in an inn.

— Belgium is the victim of the electoral census. Why nobody here wants universal suffrage.

— The Constitution is only a rag. The Constitutions are paper. Mores are the reality.

— Belgian liberty is a word. It is on paper, but it doesn't exist, because nobody needs it.

— Freedom is a decree without reason.

— Comical situation of the House at a certain moment. The two equal parties, *minus one vote*. *A splendid performance* of elections, as described by the French newspapers.

— Depiction of an electoral assembly. — Political chatter, gossip. — Political eloquence. Emphasis. Disproportion between speech *&* topic.

225. BRUSSELS
POLITICS

There are no Belgian people. Thus, when I say *the Belgian people*, it is an abbreviation that means: the different races that make up the population of Belgium.

226. BRUSSELS
GENERAL TRAITS

Homunculosity of Belgium.

This *homunculus*, the result of an alchemical operation of diplomacy, believes itself to be a man.

The fatuity of the infinitely petty.

The tyranny of the weak.
Women.
Children.
Dogs.
Belgium.

227. BRUSSELS
POLITICAL CUSTOMS

Antwerp wants to be free. Ghent wants to be free. Everyone wants to be free. And every burgomaster wants to be King.

As many Parties as cities.

As many Kermesses as Streets. Because there are Street Parties.

228. Issue about Antwerp
Fortifications
[Press clipping from *La Paix* (July 31, 1864) about the emptying of a large cemetery by a general that commanded his soldiers to disinter the bodies in order to use the site as a fortification. There is fear of unleashing the dormant cholera, which could further devastate the population. Also discussed is the war budget and maintaining an army of 100,000 men in perpetuity.]

229. BRUSSELS
   POLITICS

The Brabant Revolution & the French Revolution in Belgium.

The Brabant Revolution hostile to the French Revolution.

Misunderstanding.

[King] Joseph II leaned more toward us. A utopian at least!

The question still remains. The Brabant Revolution is clerical.

The meetings are a moronic version of the French Revolution.

Ingratitude of the Belgians for the French Republic and the Empire. —

230. BRUSSELS
   Politics

A constitutional king is an automaton in an inn.

231. BRUSSELS
   POLITICS

Belgium is the trestle of the poll tax. What would have become of France, if it had lowered the census? Constitutional retardation.

The poll tax stands at 30 fr.

Universal suffrage would put France at the mercy of priests. That's why the Liberals don't want it.

Still the great question of the Constitution (written paper) < dead letter >) and of customs (living constitution).

In France, tyranny in law, tempered by the gentleness and freedom of mores.

---

232. BRUSSELS
POLITICAL CUSTOMS

In France, freedom is limited by the fear of governments. —

— In Belgium, it's suppressed by national stupidity.

— Is it possible to be free, and what use can [a decree constituting] a decree of freedom be in a country where no one understands it, [and] where no one wants it, where no one needs it?

Freedom is an object of luxury, like virtue. When the Belgian is sated, what more does he need? *Come to Mexico, there'll be some lamb.*

233. Amusements

> [Press clipping from printer-publisher Josse Sacré informing candidates that he can print election flyers at unbeatable prices. Baudelaire marks this line: "We print for all opinions." then writes in the margin: *Nice guarantee of freedom! It seems that they do not always print for all opinions.*]

234. POLITICS

> Current comedy of the House.
> Two parties, almost equal.
> [The minority]
> The majority has one more vote.
> They canvassed the sick.
> One of those patients dies.
>
> [Here is the] Great speech over the grave of the deceased. (Lugubrious pomposity of the Protestants.)
>
> The last resort of the party lacking one vote to become the majority — is to *cast a spell* over one member of the opposing party.
>
> Never a rifle shot.
>
> Ah! If they were arguing over the price of beer, it might be very different.
>
> But this people doesn't fight for ideas. It doesn't like them.

235. BRUSSELS
GENERAL CHARACTERISTICS
POLITICS

Bombast. Military metaphors. Disproportion between speech & subject matter.

236. BRUSSELS
POLITICS

The Commercial Union only wants to elect traders.
The elector of Rue Haute.
The bootblacks (Paris).
The represented professions.

237. BRUSSELS
POLITICS
ELECTORAL ASSEMBLIES

Free meeting. Description of Bochart. Wearing a hat. He lights the lamps. — No one dares to speak. — Abolition of *everything*. The Royal Navy. —

Liberal Meeting. All the speakers: *I said.* — A punch in the stomach.
Beautiful language and clever man.

Much hullabaloo; for *nothing*; — the breach, the Flag, — punches, foam, drool: — the assembly applauds everything, — especially the last speaker. (This shows how the stupidity of this people resembles the stupidity of every nation.)

Discussions about [the Election] the *Lacroix* candidature. — Description of Lacroix.

238. *Political chattering*

>Congress of Liège.
>*Students* come together to change *education*.
>Is the little boys' convention coming soon?
>Is the congress of fetuses coming soon?

239. CONGRESS AND CHATTERING
POLITICAL MORES

>Toast to Eve.
>Toast to Cain.

240. 21. THE ANNEXATION

Annexation is a subject of conversation for the Belgians. It was the first word that I heard here, two years ago. By dint of talking about it, they forced our [sheep] <parrots> of the French press to [take care to] repeat the word.

A large part of Belgium desires it. France would have to consent to it first. A beggar cannot jump on a rich man's back and say to him: Adopt me!

I am against the annexation. There are already enough imbeciles in France, not to mention all of our former annexed peoples. Should we therefore adopt the entire universe?

But I wouldn't be against an invasion or a *Razzia*, as in earlier ages, à la Attila. Everything beautiful could be brought to the Louvre. All of which belongs to us more legitimately than to Belgium, since she no longer understands any of it. And then the Belgian ladies would make acquaintance with the Turkos <, who aren't choosy. >[57]

Belgium is a *shit-covered stick*; that is above all what constitutes its inviolability. *Don't touch Belgium!* — (Of the tyranny of the weak, animals, children, and women, that is what creates the tyranny of Belgium in European opinion.)

Belgium is preserved by a balance of rivalries. But if the rivals got along with each other! In that case, what would happen?

(Put the rest in the *Epilogue*, with conjectures on the future *&* the advice to the French.)

241. ABOUT THE ANNEXATION

The annexation, never!
There are already enough imbeciles in France.

---

242. AGAINST THE ANNEXATION

There are already enough imbeciles in France.

243. *The Annexation*

Belgium is preserved by a balance of rivalries.
But if the rivals got along!

244. 22. THE ARMY

is comparatively larger than other European armies.
But it never makes war and is not fit for marching.
< childish faces of the beardless soldiers. >

In this army, [they cannot therefore,] an officer can only hope for promotion through the natural death or suicide of a superior officer.

Great sadness among many young officers who, moreover, are educated & would make excellent soldiers.

Rhetorical exercises at the Military School. Reports of imaginary battles.

Sad comfort in inaction.

More politeness in the army than in the rest of the nation. That is not surprising. The sword ennobles and civilizes.

---

245. POLITICS
The Army

The army would like to be an army.

A huge budget for an army that doesn't fight.

All the soldiers look like children. When I see them, I think of Castelfidardo *&* the Franco-Belgian battalion.

Suicide, the means of promotion, — for the heirs of those who committed suicide.

246. BELGIUM
ARMY

In the Belgian Army, suicide is the only way forward.

Exercises of Military Rhetoric. Reports of imaginary battles.

247. 23. KING LÉOPOLD I. His portrait.
Anecdotes. His death. Mourning.

Léopold I, a miserable little German prince, went on his merry way his whole life. He didn't go into exile in a Fiacre. <Born in sabots,> he died with [several] <hundred> millions, among a European apotheosis. <Those last days, he was declared immortal.>

A type of mediocrity, but with perseverance & peasant-like cunning, that youngest of the Saxe-Coburgs, duped everybody, made his money, and in the end stole the praises that are given only to hero͂es.

Opinion of Napoléon I about him. (Ridiculous panegyric about the King in *L'Indépendance* by Mr. Considérant.)[58]

His avarice, his rapacity. — His stupid German ideas about etiquette. His relations with his sons. His pensions. The pension he received from Napoléon III.

Anecdote about the gardener.

His ideas about parks and gardens, which made him be taken for a lover of simple nature, but it was only due to his avarice.

The newspapers were falsified so that the King could read nothing alarming about his illness.

What one morning the Minister of the Interior says behind me. Ridiculous reluctance of the King to die. He steals from his mistress.

Invasion of the Duchess of Brabant & her children. She forcibly puts a crucifix to his mouth.

Traits of conformity between the death of the King and all dead Belgians. His three chaplains dispute his corpse. Mr. Becker prevails, for he speaks better French.

The great Comedy of Mourning begins. Black banners, panegyrics, apotheoses (ˣ), [piss] drinkeries, pisseries, [shit] vomitterias. Never before, *actually*, had Brussels seen such a *party*. The new King made his entry to the tune of *The Bearded King who Comes Forward*, by Offenbach. <This is a beautiful [rip] riposte to>

(ˣ) Drinkeries, pisseries, vomitterias of the whole population. — All the Belgians are in the Street, with their noses in the air, closed & silent as at a masked ball. — That's how they have fun. Never had Brussels, *actually*, seen such a *party*. — The death of its *first King*. The new King makes his entrance to the tune of *The Bearded King who Comes Forward*. Nobody laughs. — The Belgians are singing. *Let us be soldiers*, a fine retort to the annexing *fransquillons*.[59]

248. THE KING OF THE BELGIANS

A type of mediocrity, but with perseverance. He went on his merry little way his whole life. This Saxe-Coburg cadet *"came in sabots"* and died in a palace with a fortune of 100 million. — That is the true type of baseness made for success.

Finally, the great European Justice of the Peace has *laid down his knife and fork*.

"A worthless officer," replied Napoléon, at a request from Léopold, imploring to become his *aide-de-camp*.

249. BRUSSELS

> The King
> His savings.
> His avarice.
> His rapacity. The income of Napoléon III.
> Why he passes for a student of Courbet.

> His petty German prince ideas. Outdated German stupidity from another age.

> His relations with his sons.

> The Gardener.

> The sentiments of the *people* toward the King.

250. *Hardness and stupidity of the King*

Relative anecdote about the Gardener.

The King's ideas on etiquette are petty German prince ideas.

His relations with his sons.

251. BRUSSELS
POLITICS

King Léopold and his children received an indemnity from Emperor Napoléon III for their part, which disappeared from the fortune seized from the princes of Orleans. (Inform myself of the truth of this.)
Are those Orleans infamous enough & worshippers of Moloch?

BRUSSELS
The insipidness of life.

252. THE KING OF THE BELGIANS

"*Yielding to the necessities of politics,*" said Considérant, when it is a matter of justifying Léopold's baseness; — [as Lord Va] in the biography composed in provincial academic style by Considérant, everything, in Léopold, becomes a sign of genius. As Mr. Vapereau notes, making the biography of Lord Vapereau, all his moves are actions of splendor.

253. ABOUT THE KING

How and why newspapers were expurgated for the Dying King.

How foolish is a man who finds it humiliating to die! — who is offended at dying, — and who calls [sinis] sincere doctors insolents.

254. BRUSSELS
THE KING

Reluctance of the King [for] to die.
How he treats his doctors.

Great sign of imbecility in that recalcitrance against Death and in that love of life.
At what date would he fix his death if he could?

Always brutal, he had expulsed the doctor who warned him that his case was serious.

255. ABOUT THE KING'S DEATH

Since the King pretended not to be ill, they made sure to print special newspaper issues that, far from speaking of his death throes, spoke only of his recovery, so that only he would not know that he was going to die.

Mourning. Closed shops, closed theaters, black banners. Mourning, pretext for parties. All the people drink; the streets are flooded with urine. Mourning while making water without end.

What would the people of Paris do if they remained idle for eight days?

256. THE DEATH OF THE KING

I hear behind me on Rue de Louvain the Minister of the Interior, three days before the death:

"Those are tributes <(in regard to the prayers)> rendered to the *Roy-awl-tee*; but the dead *Kieng*, the Protestant, is the only thing left, — and that will be a great embarrassment."

Explanation: The three chaplains — Lutheran, Calvinist, and Anglican — <tear,> each one <tearing> a piece of the King's corpse for himself.

Thus the death of the King has a mark of conformity with all dead Belgians.

Always the corpse of Patroclus, always Mr. Wiertz.

Another question: Will he be buried in Læken or in England? This last case would not be proof of a good patriot.

257. ABOUT THE KING

The three chaplains.

The Belgians turn everything into a celebration, even the death of the King.

The bistros are full.

The people remain a week without doing anything.

What would happen to Parisians if they remained idle for eight days? We would do evil, [at least] with ardor.

And what enjoyment to draw from the cannon-shot for a week! The Belgians believe themselves to be true artillerymen.

The Avarice of the King

100 million in inheritance. The result of the most diligent avarice.

How he was treated as the husband of Princess Charlotte — paid until his death.

His savings on the maintenance of castles (Courbet).

His conduct toward Mrs. & Mr. Meyer.

---

258. ABOUT THE KING'S DEATH

The way Belgians express their mourning. — Drunkenness, pissing, vomiting. — A crowd of silent onlookers. — All noses in the air.

The new King is enthroned to the tune of *The Bearded King who Comes Forward*. No one is surprised by it.

The quip of Neyt about the death of Léopold I: *What a lucky shot for the cabarets!* [60]

A portrait of Léopold I. The [100] million. The petty pride of the German prince. [The] Madame Meyer. Vapereau and Considérant. [61]

259. 24. FINE ARTS

In Belgium, no art. It fled the Country.

No artists, — except Rops, — & Leys.

Composition, something unknown. To paint only what one sees, philosophy à la Courbet. — Specialists. — One painter for the sun, one for snow, one for moonlight, one for furniture, one for fabric, <one for flowers>, — & subdivisions of specialties to infinity, <as in industry.> <The necessary collaboration.>

[Ignoble subj] National taste for the ignoble. The old painters are therefore true historians of the Flemish spirit. — Here the emphasis doesn't exclude stupidity. — See Rubens, a louse dressed in satin.

— Some modern painters. <Understudies.> — The taste of amateurs. <Crabbe and Van Praet.>[62] How to make a collection. — The Belgians measure the value of artists by the price of their paintings.

A few pages on the infamous *charlatan* named Wiertz, the passion of English cockneys.

Analysis of the Brussels Museum. — Contrary to received opinion, the Rubens were much inferior to those in Paris.

260. *Poor Belgium*

Flemish painting.

Flemish painting only differentiates itself through qualities that are not intellectual. No spirit, but sometimes rich color, & almost always great craftsmanship. No composition. Or ridiculous composition. Ignorant subjects: pissers, shitters, & vomitters. Disgusting and monotonous jokes, which are all the spirit of the race. Types of frightening ugliness. These poor people [have depicted themselves with great talent] have put a lot of talent into [cop] copying their [monstrosity] deformity.

In that race, Rubens represents *the emphasis, which does not exclude stupidity*. Rubens is a louse dressed in satin.

261. BRUSSELS
MODERN PAINTING

Love of specialization.

There is an artist to paint the peonies.

An [A man] artist is blamed for wanting to paint everything.

How, it is said, can he know something since he doesn't focus on anything?

Because here, one must be heavy to pass for serious.

262. MODERN BELGIAN PAINTING

Art has fled the country.
Roughness in art.
Thorough painting of all that is not alive.
Painting of cattle.
Philosophy of Belgian painters. Philosophy of our friend Courbet, the interested poisoner (to paint only what one sees, so *you* will paint only what *I* see).

Verbœckhoven. (Calligraphy. A remarkable quip on *numbers*.) (Carle & Horace Vernet.)

Portæls. (Educated; no natural art. I think he knows it.)

Van der Hecht.

Dubois. (Innate feeling. Doesn't know anything about drawing.)

Rops. (About Namur. Study a lot.)

Marie Collart (very curious).

Joseph Stevens.

[Arthur] \<Alfred\> Stevens (prodigious *fragrance* of painting. Shy. — Paints *for amateurs*).

Willems.

Wiertz.	Composition is therefore
Leys.	something unknown.
Keyser (!)	The pleasure I had
Gallait (!)	to review engravings
	by Carracci.

263. PAINTING

There are literary painters, very literary. But there are pig painters (see all Flemish impurities, which, no matter how well depicted, injure the taste).

In France, they find me too painterly.
Here, they find me too literary.

Everything beyond the scope of these painters' minds they call literary art.

---

264. FINE ARTS

The way the Belgians discuss the value of paintings. Numbers, always numbers. It lasts three hours. When they have been recounting the selling prices for three hours, they believe they have had discussions about painting.

And then, you have to hide the paintings, to give them value. The eyes wear out the picture.

Everyone here is a picture dealer.

In Antwerp, if you are good for nothing you become a painter.

Always petty painting. Contempt for the great.

265. BRUSSELS
FINE ARTS

Messrs. Belgians ignore great art, decorative painting. As a matter of great art [paint] (which may have existed in the Jesuit churches in the past), there is little here but *municipal* painting (always municipal, the commune), that is to say, in short, anecdotal painting in large proportions.

266. BRUSSELS
FINE ARTS

> The exhibition, Place du Trône.
> Chenevard.
> Courbet.
> Steinle.
> Janmot.
> Kaulbach.
> Great frieze.
> Blücher.
> The king.

267- [Press clipping and statement about the death of
268. Antoine Wiertz, which the paper announces with profound emotion. Wiertz was an extraordinary man who was one of the most profound and generous

thinkers of all time. He died as he lived, "as a free thinker, and without the help of the clergy." This clipping is glued to the back of the funeral invitation Baudelaire received.]

269. BRUSSELS
PAINTING

> Wiertz shares stupidity with Doré & Victor Hugo. The madmen are too stupid (Bignon).

270r*–v.* BRUSSELS
MODERN PAINTING

> *Independent* Painting.

Wiertz. Charlatan. Idiot, thief. He believes he has a destiny to accomplish.

Wiertz the literary painter <philosopher>. Modern nicknames. The Christ of the humanitarians. Philosophical painting. Stupidity analogous to that of Victor Hugo at the end of the *Contemplations*. Abolition of the death penalty. Infinite power of man [comm]. The crowds of brass.

The captions on the walls. Great insults against French critics and France. The sentences of Wiertz everywhere. Mr. Gagne. Utopias. Brussels the capital of the world. Paris a province. Bignon's phrase on the stupidity of madmen.

Wiertz's books. Plagiarism. He doesn't know how to draw, and his stupidity is as great as his colossal figures.

In short, this charlatan knew how to do his business. But what will Brussels do with all that after his death?

The Trompe-l'œil.
The Soufflet.
Napoléon in Hell.
The Lion of Waterloo.
Wiertz *&* V. Hugo want to save humanity.

[No entry for 271]

272. MUSEUMS. Museum of Brussels

Vanthulden's roughness. Rolling back of the septuagenarians. Flemish dirt (always the pisser and the vomitter). Thus what I used to take for the caprices of the imagination of a few artists is a true translation of customs. (Lovers who kiss each other by vomiting.)

Van den Plas and *Pierre Meert*.

Pictures as badly labeled as in France.

Mirrors of *Philippe de Champagne*.

A *Canaletto* Canal.

Tintoretto (Madeleine perfuming the feet of Jesus).

Paul Veronese. Sketch. Synopsis of the *Last Supper* of the Louvre.

Veronese. The presentation.

Veronese. A shower of crowns (recalling Veronese's ceiling of the Grand Salon).

Guardi, labeled *Canaletto*.

A beautiful portrait of *Titian*.

A pleasant *Albane*, the first I see.

Preti. Rape, battle, punctured eye.

Tintoretto. Shipwreck at the bottom of a palace (see Catalog).

Metzu. Cuyp. Maas. Téniers. Palamède.

Beautiful *Van der Neer*. *Ryckaert* (makes one think of *The Dwarf*).

Superb *Meert. Janssens*. Superb *Jordaens*.

Rembrandt (cold). *Ruysdael* (sad).

Curious sketch of Rubens, very white.

Superb Rubens. The buttocks of the Venus, astonished but flattered by the audacity of the satyr who kisses them.

Peter Neefs. Gothic church, already adorned with statues and Jesuit altars.

David Téniers (very beautiful).

David Téniers.

Backhuysen (banal).

Portrait of a woman, an honest woman à la Maintenon, by Bol.

Jan Steen. 2 paintings, including a very beautiful one. Flemish fools *&* scoundrels.

274- MUSEUM OF BRUSSELS
275.

Van Dyck, Hairdresser for Ladies.

Silène, superb painting, labeled *Van Dyck*, to be rightly credited to *Jordaens.*

Jordaens. The Satyr *&* the Peasant.

(Jordaens is more personal and more candid than Rubens. Rubens' fatuousness, and overwhelmingly happy people, are unbearable to me.) (The blandness of continuous happiness *&* pink.)

Isabel Clara Eug. Hisp. Belg. and burg. prin.
Albertus archid. Austriæ belg. and burg. prin.

Decorative portraits a little larger than life. Superb Rubens, *curious* Rubens.

Emmanuel Biset.
Ehrenberg-Emelraet (see Catalog).
Hubert Goltzius.
Smeyers (composer. A rare thing here).
Siberechts (reminiscent of *Le Nain*).
Jordaens an exorcism.

Jordaens a triumph.

In connection with the great Rubens in the background:

I knew Rubens perfectly well before coming here.
Rubens, Decadence. Rubens, anti-religious.
Rubens, drab. Rubens, a fountain of banality.
Wonderful richness of the Museum, in fact of *primitives*.

Sturbant (?).
Roger of Bruges. Charles the Bold.
Holbein (The Little Dog).
The famous panels of *Van Eyck*. (Stunning, but clownishly Flemish.)

Velvet Brueghel.
Brueghel the Old? (See Arthur)
Brueghel the Comic
(Massacre of the innocents, a town in winter, soldiers' entrance, white ground, Persian silhouettes.)
Mabuse. The perfumes of Madeleine.
Van Orley. — Van Eyck.

Fortunately for me, we didn't see the moderns.

276. 25. ARCHITECTURE — CHURCHES. WORSHIP

Modern civil architecture. — No harmony. — Architectural incongruities. — Good materials. < The blue stone. > — Fragility of the houses. —

Trash. — Pastiches of the past. — In the monuments, counterfeits of France. — In the churches, counterfeits of the past.

The passé. The Gothic. The 17th C.

Description of the Grand Place of Brussels (very neat).

— In Belgium, always late, styles linger and last longer.

— In praise of 17th-C. style, unknown style, and of which there are magnificent samples in Belgium. —Renaissance in Belgium. — Transition. — Jesuit style. — Styles from the 17th C. — Rubens Style.

— *Beguinage* churches in Malines, Jesuit churches in Brussels, *St. Pierre* churches in Malines, *Jesuit* churches in Antwerp, *Saint-Loup* churches in Namur, etc., etc....

(The reaction of V. Hugo in favor of the Gothic is very detrimental to our understanding of architecture, and we have lingered in it too long.) — Philosophy of the history of architecture, *in my opinion*. Analogies with corals, *madrepores*, the formation of the continents, and finally the modes of creation in universal life. — Never gaps. — Permanent state of transition. — It may be said that the Rococo is the last flowering of the Gothic.

— Cobergher, Faid'herbe, and Franquart.[63] — Opinion of Joly on Cobergher, still derived from Victor Hugo.

— General wealth of churches. A little shop of curiosities, — a little junk. Description of that kind of wealth.

— Some churches, either Gothic or 17th C. My taste for veneers, blends. It's history.

— Colored statues. Very decorated confessionals. — At the Beguinage, Antwerp, Malines, Namur, etc. — The Chairs of Truth. Very varied. — The true Flemish sculpture is made of wood and is mostly found in churches. — Sculpture not sculptural, not monumental, childish, <trinket> sculpture, sculpture of patience. Moreover, that art is dead like the others, even in Malines.

— Description of some processions. Traces of the past, still subsisting in religious manners. Great luxury. Astonishing naiveté in the dramatization of religious ideas. (Observe, by the way, the countless number of Belgian parties, always a celebration, a great sign of popular idleness.)

— Belgian devotion. Dumb. Superstition. The Christian God is not within reach of the Belgian Brain.

— The Clergy: heavy, coarse, cynical, lubricious, rapacious. In a word, *Belgian*. It was he who made the Revolution in 1831, and he believes that all Belgian life belongs to him.

— Let us return a little to the Jesuits *&* the Jesuit style. Style of genius. The ambiguous and complex character of that style.

— Coquettish and terrible. Large openings, great light, a mixture of figures, styles, ornaments, and symbols. I saw tiger legs serving as windings!

— Some examples. Generally poor churches outside, except on the facade.

277. BRUSSELS
ARCHITECTURE

A pot & a rider on a roof are the most prominent evidence of extravagant taste in architecture. A horse on a roof! A pot of flowers on a pediment!

That refers to what I call the *toy* style.

Muscovite bell towers. On a Byzantine bell tower, a bell, or rather a doorbell, — which makes me want to detach it to ring for my servants, — giants.

The beautiful houses of the *Grand Place* recall the curious furniture called *Lavatories*. Childish style.

The rest of the fine pieces of furniture are always from small monuments.

278. BRUSSELS
   ARCHITECTURE. SCULPTURE

   Pots on the roofs.
   (Destination of the pots.)
   An equestrian statue on a roof. Here is a man galloping on the roofs.
   In general, unintelligent sculpture, except childish sculpture, ornamental sculpture, where they are very strong.

---

279. ARCHITECTURE

   In general, ingenious and coquettish, even in modern constructions. Absence of classical proportions.
   The blue stone.

   The Grand Place.
   Before the bombardment of Villeroi, even now, prodigious decor. Coquettish and solemn. — The equestrian statue. Emblems, busts, various styles, gold, pediments, the house attributed to Rubens, caryatids, the back of a ship, the Town Hall, the King's house, a world of paradoxes, architecture. Victor Hugo (see Dubois *&* Wauters).

   The wharf at the barracks.

280- [*Notes in someone else's handwriting relating to the*
281. *Grand Place of Brussels.*]

282. *Brussels*
Architecture & backward litterateurs

> Cobergher and Victor Joly.
> "If I took this Cobergher!" said Joly, — "a wretch who has corrupted the religious style!"
> The existence of Cobergher, architect of the church of the Beguinage, the Augustinians, and the Brigantines, was revealed to me by *Magasin pittoresque*. In vain I had asked several Belgians the architect's name.
> V. Joly has remained at *Notre-Dame de Paris*. — "He cannot pray," — he said, — "in a Jesuitical church." — "He needs a Gothic one."
> There are idlers who find in the color of the curtains of their room a reason for never working.

283. BRUSSELS AND BELGIAN ARCHITECTURE

> General character of the churches.
> Sometimes real wealth, sometimes junk.
> Just as the houses of the Grand Place look like curious furniture, so churches often look like boutique curiosities.

But that's not unpleasant. Childish honors returned to the Lord.

---

284. BRUSSELS
GENERAL CHARACTERISTICS
WORSHIP

A second procession, about the miracle of the stabbed host.
Large painted statues.
Colorful crucifixes.
Beauty of painted sculpture.
The eternal Crucified above the crowd. — Bushes of artificial roses.
My tenderness.

Fortunately, I didn't see the faces of the people who carried those magnificent images.

285. CHURCHES. BRUSSELS

Sainte-Gudule. Magnificent stained glass windows. Beautiful intense colors, like those that a profound soul projects onto all the objects of life.

Saint Catherine. Exotic perfume. Ex-votos. Painted, disguised, end adorned virgins. Specific odor of wax *&* incense.

Always enormous and theatrical chairs. Staging in wood. Beautiful industry, which makes you want to order furniture in Malines or Leuven.

The churches always closed, past the time of the offices. We must therefore pray *on time, as the Prussian.*

Tax on tourists.

When you enter at the end of the office, with a gesture you are shown a table where one reads:
. . . .

286. BRUSSELS

> The Belgian Religions
> Atheism.
> Allan Kardec.[64]
> A religion that satisfies the heart and mind.

A people who never find their religion beautiful enough for them.

287. ARCHITECTURE. JESUIT STYLE

A brave bookseller who prints books against priests and nuns, and who probably learns from the books he prints, assures me that there is no Jesuit style, [—in] — in [where] <that> the Jesuits have covered their monuments.

288- CHURCHES. BRUSSELS
289.

>Try to define the Jesuit style.
>Composite style.
>Coquettish barbarism.
>The failures.
>Charmingly bad taste.
>Chapel of Versailles.
>Collège de Lyon.
>The Boudoir of Religion.
>Great glories.
>Mourning in marble (black & white).
>Solomonic columns.
>(Rococo) statues suspended from capital columns, even Gothic columns.
>Ex-votos. (Large ship.)

A church made of varied styles is a historical dictionary. It's the natural wastefulness of history.

Painted, disguised, & adorned Madonnas.

Tumular stones. Funereal sculptures appended to the columns. (J.-B. Rousseau)

Extraordinary rococo chairs, dramatic confessionals. In general, a domestic style of sculpture, & the chairs done in a childish style.

The chairs are a world of emblems, a pompous tohu-bohu of religious symbols, sculpture [represented] by a skillful chisel from Malines or Louvain.

Palm trees, oxen, eagles, griffins; Sin, Death, putti, instruments of the passion, Adam & Eve, the Crucifix, foliage, rocks, curtains, etc., etc.

In general, a gigantic painted crucifix, suspended in the vault before the choir of the great nave (?).

(I love painted sculpture.)

That is what a photographer of my friends calls Jesus Christ doing the trapeze.

290. CHURCHES. BRUSSELS

Jesuit churches. Flamboyant Jesuit style. Rococo Religion, old impressions from books to prints. The miracles of the Paris Deacon. (Jansenism, watch out.)

The Beguinage church. Delicious impression of whiteness. The Jesuitical churches, very airy, very enlightened.

That one has all the snowy beauty of a young communicant.

Pots à feu, dormers, busts in niches, winged heads, statues perched on capitals.

Charming confessionals.

Religious coquetry.

The cult of Mary, very beautiful in all the churches.

291. CHURCHES. BRUSSELS

Church of *the Chapel*.

A painted crucifix, and below, *Nuestra Señora de la Soledad* (Our Lady of Solitude).

Beguine costume. Great mourning, big black & white sails, black muslin dress.

As great as nature.

Gold tiara inlaid with glass beads.

Gold halo with rays of light.

Heavy rosary, smelling of its convent.

The face is painted.

Terrible color, terrible Spanish style.

(De Quincey, the Notre-Dame.)[65]

A <white> skeleton leaning out of a black marble grave hanging from the wall.

(More astonishing than that of Saint-Nicolas du Chardonnet.)

292. 26. THE LANDSCAPE

— Fatty, copious, [li] humid, like the
woman, dark as the man.

— Very black greenery.
— Climate wet, cold, hot, & humid: the four seasons in one day.

— Life scarce in the woods and in the meadows. The animal itself avoids those cursed regions.

— No insects, no songbirds.

293. BRUSSELS
[Characteristics]
GENERAL CHARACTERISTICS OF
THE NEARBY COUNTRY

Bold, rich, and dark aspect of the surroundings of Brussels. Overripe, but dark vegetation. Wet mist. Nature similar to that of the inhabitants.

Wonderful culture. Everything is cultivated. [Horticultural] activity of the plowman. They cultivate inclined areas with the spade and the pickaxe.

Yet in those rich, ignoble, filthy, yellowish areas of the countryside, children surround you in groups & beg obstinately with an exasperating song. They are not the children of the poor. — Parents, rich farmers sometimes, sometimes, intervene in this way: *Oh! The little greedy ones, they want to have some cake.*

And these people claim to be free!

It's necessary to pay a fee to each border, that is to say all the ..... Feudal debris. The borders are leased.

294. BRUSSELS
GENERAL CHARACTERISTICS

The beauty of the Quai des Barques, and the Green Alley.

Duckweed and grass with ducks. Unusual, sudden invasion. — A green carpet, which makes you want to walk on it, but which removes the beauty of the moiré of the waters.

295.
27. WALK TO MALINES
28. WALK TO ANTWERP
29. WALK TO NAMUR

MALINES. Malines is a good little hooded beguine. Mechanical music in the air. Every day resembles Sunday. Crowds in the Churches. Grass in the Streets. <Old Spanish Stench.> <The Beguinage.> Several Churches. Saint-Rombaud. Our Lady.

Saint Pierre. Paintings of two Jesuit brothers. Continuous confessional. Wonderful symbol of the pulpit, the only sculptural sculpture that I've seen. — Smell of wax and incense. — Rubens and Van Dyck. — Botanical Garden. — Good wine from Moselle at Hôtel de la Levrette. — The particular society. — The Marseillaise carillon.

ANTWERP. Appearance of the Archbishop of Malines. Flat country, black greenery. — New (!) & ancient fortifications with English gardens. Finally, here is a city that has the great air of a capital. The place of Meir. The House of Rubens. The House of the King. Flemish Renaissance. City Hall. — The Church of the Jesuits. Masterpiece. Still in the style of the Jesuits (hodgepodge, chessboard, golden chandeliers. <Glory and transparency, angels & cupids, apotheoses and beatifications> — Mourning in marble. — Theatrical confessionals. — Confessional Theater. — Mystical & [sinister] terrible boudoir). What I think of the famous Rubens, the closed churches & sacristans.> — Calvaries & Madonnas. — Majesty of Antwerp. Beauty of a great river. <The basins> <Antwerp seen from the river.> — Mr. Leys. — Plantin's house. — Prostitution in Antwerp <a large brothel in the suburbs.> As everywhere, closed Churches & the rapacity of the sacristans. — Coarse manners. <Funereal air of restaurant boys.> — [Polit] Antwerp policy. <[The basins]>

NAMUR. <We're not going there.> Village of Vauban, of Boileau, of Van der Meulen, of Bossuet, of Fénelon, of Jouvenet, of Restout, of Rigaud, etc. ... [Impression] <Memories> of *Lutrin*. — Saint-Loup. The masterpiece of the Jesuits. The Recollects. Saint-Aubin, Saint-Pierre of Rome in bricks and blue stone. — Nicolai, false Rubens. — The street of blind finches. — Prostitution. — Walloon populations. More politeness. Portrait of Rops and his father-in-law, a unique man, a severe and jovial magistrate, <a great quoter and> a great hunter. <The only man in Belgium who knows Latin and looks like a Frenchman.> I go to Luxembourg without knowing it. <The landscape, black; the Meuse, steep & foggy. The wine in Namur.>

296- MALINES
297.

    Botanical Garden.

    General impression of rest, festivity, devotion.

    Mechanical music in the air. It [expresses] <represents> the joy of a mechanical people who can only divert themselves with discipline. The chimes keep the individual from finding an expression of his or her joy.

— In Malines, every day seems like a Sunday.

An old Spanish stench.

Saint-Rombaud (Raimbault, Rombauld) Gothic. Church of St. Peter.
History of St. Francis Xavier painted by two brothers, painters & Jesuits, & symbolically echoed on the facade.
One of them prepares his paintings in red.
Theatrical style à la Restout.
Character of the Jesuit Churches. Light and whiteness.
These churches always seem to commune.
All of St. Peter's is surrounded by pompous confessionals, which continue without interruption, and form a broad belt of the most ingenious, most rich, & most bizarre sculptured symbols.
The Jesuit church is summarized in the Pulpit. The globe of the world. The four parts of the world. Louis of Gonzaga, Stanislas Kostka, Francis Xavier, St. Françoise Régis.
Old women and beguines. Mechanical devotion. Perhaps true happiness. A strong odor of wax & incense, absent from Paris, an emanation found only in the villages. Halles of Drapiers. Flemish Louis XVI.

298. MALINES

Malines is traversed by a rapid and [clear] green stream. But sleeping Malines is not a nymph; it is a *béguine* [béguine] whose gaze [prud] hardly <dares> to [slip] out of the darkness> of the hood.

She is a little old woman, not afflicted, not tragic, but nevertheless sufficiently mysterious to the eye of the stranger, not [accustomed to the minuti] <familiar with the> solemn minutiæ of devout life.

(Religious paintings, — devotees, but not believers, — according to Michelangelo).

. . . .

Profane airs adapted to chimes. Through airs that crossed [, in] and commingled, it seemed to me to seize some notes from *La Marseillaise*. The Hymn of the Canaille, rushing from the belltowers, lost a little of its harshness. Ruined by the hammers, [it was losing a bit of] [it was not traditional ululating], [<according to tradition]> it was no longer the great traditional ululation, but <it> seemed to take on some childlike grace. One would have said that the Revolution was learning to stutter the language of Heaven. Heaven, clear and blue, received, without vexation, that homage of the earth confounded with the [...] <others>.

299- FIRST VISIT TO ANTWERP
301.

Departure from Brussels. What joy! Mr. Neyt. The Archbishop of Malines. Flat country. Black greenery. (The ululations of a worker.)

News and ancient fortifications of Antwerp. English gardens on the fortifications. The place of Meir. The House of Rubens. — The King's House.

Ancient Styles. Flemish Renaissance. Rubens Style. Jesuit style.

Renaissance Flanders: City Hall of Antwerp. (Coquetry, sumptuousness, pink marble, gold.)

Jesuit Style: Jesuit Church of Antwerp.

Church of the Beguinage in Brussels. Very composite style. Hodgepodge of styles. Chessboard. — Golden chandeliers. — Mourning in marble, — black and white. Theatrical confessionals. There is drama and boudoir in Jesuit decoration. Industry of wooden sculpture, Malines and Louvain.

Catholic luxury in the most sacristan *&* boudoir sense.

Coquetry of Religion.

The Calvaries *&* the Madonnas.

Chic modern style of the architecture of the houses. Blue granite. Mixture of renaissance and moderate rococo.

Cape Town style.

Town Hall (pink *&* gold marble).

In Antwerp, we breathe, at last!

Majesty and breadth of the Scheldt. The Great Basins. Channels or basins for coasting.

Fairground music nearby the ships. Serendipity.

Church of St. Paul. Gothic exterior. Jesuit interior. Pompous, theatrical confessionals. Side chapels in marble colors. Chapel of the Collège de Lyon. (Ridiculous Calvary. Here the dramatic sculpture reaches wild comedy, involuntary comedy.)

(The Church of the Béguinage in Brussels.)

Our Lady of Antwerp. The pomp of Quentin Metzys, James Tissot.

Rapidity of the sacristans. Paintings of Rubens restored and retained in the sacristy to derive the greatest possible profit. 1 fr. (per person). If a French priest dared to …

The kitchen in Antwerp.

Herring Canal, or the famous Rydeck.

Prostitution.

Wonderful aspect of the capital. Manners coarser than in Brussels, more Flemish.

302- *Trip to Namur*
303.

FROM BRUSSELS TO NAMUR. — Still black greenery. [Flowery and] fertile country.

Namur. — Town of Boileau and Van der Meulen. The impression of *Boileau and Van der Meulen* remained in me the entire time of my stay. And then, after that I had visited the monuments, *Lutrin* impression. In Namur, all monuments date from Louis XIV, or at the latest from Louis XV.

Always the Jesuit [Ren] style (not by Rubens this time, nor Flemish Renaissance). Three important churches, *the Récollets, Saint-Aubin, Saint-Loup*. Once, characterize the beauty of this style (late Gothic). A particular art, composite art. In search of origins (De Brosses).

Saint-Aubin. Pantheon, St. Peter's of Rome. Bricks.

Note [the portal & pediment] the convexity of the portal & the pediment.

Beautiful grids. Solemnity of the 18th C.

Was it at *Saint-Aubin* or *Récollets* that I admired the Nicolai? What is Nicolai? Paintings by Nicolaï, engraved with Rubens' signature. *Nicolai Jesuit*. Keep working.

Saint-Loup. Sinister and gallant marvel. *Saint-Loup* differs from all that I have seen of the Jesuits.

The interior of a catafalque embroidered with black, pink, and silver. Confessional, all of a varied style: fine, subtle, baroque, a *new antiquity*. The *Beguinage* church in Brussels is a communicant. *Saint-Loup* is a terrible *&* delicious catafalque.

The general majesty of all those Jesuitical churches, flooded with light, with large windows, boudoirs of Religion, repelled by *Victor Joly*, who claims to be able to pray only under Gothic arches, — *a man who prays very little.*

Technical description (as much as possible) of Saint-Loup.

The finches. Blind people. Fishing companies. Barbarity.

Prostitution.

The featured name of the successful girl.

Sometimes printed on a lantern,

    in poor districts, written in chalk.

— A beautiful chapter on Rops. —

— Walloon population. — What is Walloon? I am mistaken about the railway. — Gaiety, fun, bantering, benevolence.

---

304. AMUSEMENTS

Mr. Kertbeny. The porters and the [Monsieur] Ciceroni on the lookout for foreigners.

"Sir, I know fifty-two languages." But he only knows fifty-one.

Sample of his style (one card).

His ideas on Bohemian music and Liszt. — < The French language is the newest language. >

— His invitation to Couty de la Pommerais.[66] — < German is a Flemish patois. — The French are wise men & gods. >

Poe is French like Mr. de Noé.

Painting of Leys an acoustic phenomenon. < Painting of Delacroix, caricature and experimental, acoustic phenomenon. > Sea sickness, acoustic phenomenon.

At the sight of the Cemetery, a tavern for Monselet, one day when I contemplated the funeral of a solidarist, and a coffin at the door of a cabaret.

305.   30. WALK IN LIÈGE
       31. WALK IN GHENT
       32. WALK IN BRUGES

LIÈGE.   The Palace of the Princes-Bishops. — Drunkenness. — Cellars. Great pretensions of the French spirit.

GHENT. Saint-Bavon. Wild population — Old city of rebels, has the airs of a capital, set apart.

BRUGES. — Phantom city, mummy town, pretty much preserved. It smells of death, the Middle Ages, Venice, the (routine) specters, the tombs. A great work attributed to Michelangelo. — Great Beguinage. Chimes.

However, Bruges is also on the way out.

306. 33. EPILOGUE — THE FUTURE
ADVICE TO THE FRENCH

Belgium is what France might have become if the electoral census had been maintained.

— Belgium is sleeping.

— Cut into sections, divided, invaded, defeated, beaten, looted, the Belgian [experience] <vegetate> still, [clean miracle] <pure> marvel of the mollusk.

— *Noli me tangere!* a beautiful Motto for her.

— Who would like to touch her?

— Belgium is a hell. Who would like to adopt her?

— However, it has in her [its] [many] elements of dissolution. The diplomatic harlequin may be dislocated from one moment to another.

— One party can go to Prussia, another to Holland, & the Wallonia provinces to France. — Great misfortune for us. Portrait of the Walloon.

— Ungovernable breeds, not due to excessive vitality, but because of the total lack of ideas and feelings. It's nothingness (Maturin quote) (*The Companion of Dumouriez*). Commercial interests in gambling, which I don't want to deal with.

One can conquer those people; tame them, never.
Always the question of annexation. <Antwerp would like to be a free city.> Small towns (Brussels, Geneva), wicked cities. Peoples (bad peoples).

Brief advice to French people condemned to live in Belgium, in order not to be too robbed, insulted, or poisoned.

307. BRUSSELS
BEGINNING

It's certain that the gloomiest prospect presents nothing so chilling as the aspect of human faces, in which we try in vain to trace one corresponding expression.

Maturin

308. POOR BELGIUM

To the critic, to the unwelcome observer, Belgium, somnolent & brutalized, would gladly reply: "I am happy; do not wake me up!"

309.

If the Belgian were cut into sections, it would still live. It's a worm that we had forgotten to crush.

It's completely stupid, but it's as resilient as a mollusk.

A hyperborean, a gnome without an eyelid, without a pupil [,] and without a forehead, and which rings in the hollow, like an empty tomb when a gun strikes it.

310. POOR BELGIUM

Belgium is a case that confirms the theory of the Tyranny of the Weak.

No one would dare touch Belgium.

Noli me tangere, a beautiful motto for her.

She is sacred.

311. BELGIUM
GENERAL CHARACTERISTICS

Having looked for much of the Belgians' *raison d'être*, I had imagined that they were perhaps old souls, locked up for horrible vices, in hideous bodies [where no] which [their] are their image.

A Belgian is the <one> hell [that exists] <lives> on earth.

312. *Poor Belgium*

It has sometimes occurred to my mind that Belgium was perhaps one of the graduated hells, scattered throughout creation, and that the Belgians were, as Kircher believes of certain animals, ancient criminal spirits [where] <and> abject beings enclosed in deformed bodies.

[It] We become Belgian for having sinned.

A Belgian is his own hell.

313. BRUSSELS

> *Destiny of Belgium*
> perhaps in the *Epilogue*

Annexation?
Dismemberment?

Nothing easier. Belgium is entirely ready. She would throw up her hands.

Nothing could be easier than conquering Belgium. Nothing could be more difficult than taming it.

And then, what about it? What is the point of [re] reducing to slavery people who don't know how to cook eggs?

314. *Politics*

    Epilogue.
    Invasion.

Belgium is what France would have become under the continued rule of Louis Philippe, a fine example of constitutional degradation.

Pride suffering from the Bœotians.
Frog people yearning to be oxen.

There are cities (Brussels, Geneva) that, like prudes, seem to excite covetousness.

This question of [the invas] the invasion is repeated in conversation.

But no one wants you, only the Devil!

315. POLITICS
About the invasion

Invasion

A country so often conquered, and which has been able, despite the frequent intrusion of strangers, to obstinately guard its customs, ought not to so frequently affect fright. This little people is much stronger than it appears to be.

---

316. BRUSSELS
POLITICS

Invasion

Annexation

Belgium doesn't want to be invaded, but she hopes that they want to invade her.
It's an oaf that wants to inspire desires.
To tell the truth, would the Walloons be upset?

317. POLITICS

Lying patriotism

Belgian Patriotism

One patriot, Victor Joly, in a country where there is no country.

His portrait.

Belgium is being auctioned. Is there a buyer at such a price? Holland doesn't say a word. Nor does France. Belgium is unmarketable. It's a shit-covered stick.

Invasion & annexation are the dreams of an old coquettish prude. She always believes that we think of her. For Belgium to be annexed, France would have to consent.

318. POOR BELGIUM
HISTORY

Razzia

The Flemings who supported the Duke of Alba, who had only ten thousand Spaniards, and only revolted during the tax of the twentieth.

Notice to any European Army. *Never annexation.* But still the *Razzia.*

[The *razzia* of]

We have to start with that. The *razzia* of monuments, paintings, art objects of all kinds.

The *razzia* of riches.

You can transport everything that is beautiful. Every nation has the right to say: *It belongs to me, since the Belgians do not enjoy it.*

---

319. BRUSSELS
     GENERAL CHARACTERISTICS
     CUSTOMS

Annexation.

Fear of annexation, but the desire that France desires it.

But they would be insulted by telling them that there is no danger for them and that France doesn't want them.

The nose of the Churchwarden —

Everything that I say about the ridiculous Flemings cannot be applied to the Walloons.

320. Annexation

[Press clipping from *Gazette belge* (Sept. 23, 1865) about Napoléon in Mexico and Prussia and England's resolution to abandon Belgium, first on the condition that they leave the Rhine provinces, and second that Antwerp be made a free port & that its fortifications be demolished so that "it cannot be left to the hands of France, a pistol pointed at the heart of its rival." "What is truly comical in all these combinations is that the imperial government, as France says, does not even intend to proceed by force." Another clipping evinces doubt regarding the duration of Belgium's national independence, then demands that every organ of the Belgian press, which should be devoted to the cause of the autonomy & freedoms of the country, seek, with great solicitude, what effects this quasicall abroad may have produced.]

321r*-v.* BRUSSELS

POLITICS

Annexation
Razzia

The annexation! always annexation! we only hear of this here.

Because the Emperor reigns here, he is the principal power, as the *Kladderadatsch* has shown (find the passage).[67]

(Three Powers: the Chamber, *Belgian Independence*, and the French Emperor.) Constitutional government, triad of powers.

The opinion of Verwee.⁶⁸ Belgium at first forgets that *the annexation is made morally*, afterwards that it would require *France's consent*. — Stop the first-comer in the street and say to him: *Be my adopted father*, especially if you are a filthy child. The eel that wants to be flayed, but screams before it is flayed. The nose of the churchwarden.

I mean then annexation: *to seize the land, buildings, and wealth, and deport all the inhabitants.* — Impossible to use them as slaves. They are too stupid.

The wickedness of small countries (Belgium, Switzerland), *the wickedness of the weak*, pugs, and hunchbacks.

After all, such circumstances may arise that divide the diplomatic harlequin in half: half for Holland, half for France.

My opinion about the Walloons.

There is only one person in the world *that dreams of annexation, and it is Belgium*. It is true that the *famous* Wiertz understood it differently.

Let the Hyperboreans return to the north!

322. POOR BELGIUM
EPILOGUE

Advice to the French.

Food.
Clothing.
Do not see anyone.
Defiance.
No familiarity.
Etc., etc.

323. UNCLASSIFIED PAGES

The landscape. The parks.
Freethinkers (the phrase of Morellet).
Literature (annalists and collectors).
Beaux-arts (the phrase of Van Præt).
Women.
The Belgian Brain (Belgian Nothingness).
Customs (compliance, family foresight.
Two enemy brothers).
Customs (<Joyous> Conformity. *The joyous.* Finches. The Duke of Brabant, president).
Customs (conformity *&* cleanliness of young girls).
Customs (improbability of merchants. Owner of Malassis).

Customs (Belgian hospitality).

Brussels (exiles & emigrants). Teachers.

Appetizers (Booth, Lincoln, Corday, the surgeon Gendrin).[69]

Brussels (the Belgians' bizarre ideas about French servitude).

Amusements (Kertbeny).[70]

Administrations. Telegraph. Post Office. Warehouse.

324r.*   The Spies.   Rudeness.
         Closed   Gallic salt.
         churches.   Shit.
         Money.
         The Beguinage.
         [The procession]
         The solidarist.   (Flags.)
         The army.   Delacroix.
         The balls.   The chairs.
         Theater.   The conf.
         The Jesuits.   Dogs.

---

cold mystification.

  Arenberg. *Van Praet.*
  Antwerp. *Gœthals.*[71]
  Bruges.
  Rops.   *Coûteaux.*[72]

324v.* [A message in Kertbeny's handwriting about having had the honor of *attacking* (his French not being perfect, he writes *"d'attenter"* instead of *"d'attendant"*) Baudelaire until midday, whose kind visit he was very happy to receive. Kertbeny also mentions the arrival of a famous painter.]

325. BELGIAN ADMINISTRATIONS

  Positions.
  Telegraph.
  Warehouse — Customs.

My adventures with L A P O S T E, about the events. No law objects that are not a correspondence (manuscripts).

Mr. Hoschtei.

The Van Gend administration (about manuscripts).

  T H E T E L E G R A P H does not deposit the dispatches. My adventures with the Telegraph.

CUSTOMS. Rudeness and stupidity of employees.

[12] 13 offices, 20 signatures from me, 20 signatures from the administration. The Comptroller of Customs. <His portrait.> The Director of Customs. The minister of the Interior. The Minister of Finance. [Minister of the Interior.] "The real reason why I brought my watch to Belgium?" — No old tribulations equal to this one.

326. Brussels

The landscape.

Nature of the Land around Brussels, muddy or sandy, preventing the ability to walk.

State of abandonment and neglect of all parks.

327. *About freethinkers*

Male freethinkers with *their* female *free* thinkers.....
Priests with *their priestesses.*
(Morellet)

328. BELGIAN LITERATURE

What is the profession of the annalist in Belgium.
— Trade of the annals.

Everybody in Belgium is a salesman. Some sell bundles of annals, others paintings.

329. FINE ARTS
BRUSSELS

Amateurs of Paintings.
Thieves [?] and merchants of paintings.

A minister, with whom I visit the gallery, said to me, as I was praising David: "*It seems to me that David is rising in value?*"

I reply: "David had never fallen in value among the wise."

---

330. *Brussels*
Women

Chickens, minxes, shrikes.

---

331. BRUSSELS
BELGIAN BRAIN

> [you]
> Belgian Nothingness.

You tell a touching or sublime story (that he died! etc. ...)

All the Belgians burst out laughing, because they believe that they must laugh.

You tell a Funny story; they look at you with wide eyes, with a distressed air.

You tease them. They feel flattered and believe in compliments.

You give them a compliment. They think you are teasing them.

332. BRUSSELS
CUSTOMS

> Providence in families.
> The father has two sons.
> One will be liberal (the elder branch).
> The other clerical (the younger branch).
> And so the future of the family is based on the two possible futures. So it cannot lose.
> It is in the two possibilities that it is pledged.

333. BRUSSELS
CUSTOMS

> Spirit of conformity, even in joy.
> Association of 40 happy men to invent April fish.

> The pupil of the finches.
> Society to poke out the eyes of finches.

> The Duke of Brabant, president of a Finchian Academy.

> Barbarism of childhood games.
> Birds attached by the foot to a stick.

334. BRUSSELS
CUSTOMS

Belgian Cleanliness

> Spirit of imitation in little girls.
> All day, little girls rubbing a small part of the sidewalk with a little rag. Future housewives.

335. BRUSSELS
CUSTOMS

    Universal Improbability

 The means of the scapegoats of merchants, very restricted; people without imagination.

 Add the number of one account to the total number of a bill.

 (Dame! Sir, we do not wish to dispute with you.)

 Two days after a bill was acknowledged, they presented it again. — I paid. — No, since this is your bill. (They hope that, as a Frenchman, you have mislaid the paid invoice, but you find it.) Then:

 — Dame! Sir, we do not want to argue with you.

 That is the conforming answer.

 Malassis' landlady.

336. BRUSSELS
CUSTOMS

 A small chapter on *Belgian hospitality*, a Belgian phrase.

 How was that prejudice made in the minds of the Belgians — and the French?

 Political exiles.

   <Adventures come to my knowledge.>

337. BRUSSELS

Belgian Hospitality

So much has been said of it that the Belgians themselves believe it.

Belgian hospitality consists in grabbing the poor, hungry Frenchmen and transporting them immediately to England,

or to well *garrison* the journalists, to insult them vigorously, and to throw them onto any frontier; <then they demanded their salary from the Emperor, who asked nothing of them.>

But if one learns that a Frenchman has money, one keeps him preciously, to eat him. Then, when he is ruined, he is thrown abruptly into prison for Debts, where new phenomena of exploitation take place (the bed, the table, the chairs, etc.).

Thus Belgian hospitality (which applies to all travelers) is political economy, or cannibalism.

338. HYGIENE

Be a *great man* for oneself.

Belgium

Administration of posts.   Flights.
(Proofs — petition to the Senate) (*Malassis*).

Telegraph.
Flight. History of my dispatch.
(*Closed house.*)
(*I kiss you.*)

Institutions derived from customs. No law for the proofs.

A people that doesn't write, and has no thoughts to communicate.

Dispatches not filed.

A people who have nothing important or urgent to say cannot believe that other peoples have anything urgent to convey.

As man makes God in his image, the Belgian people imagine other peoples being like them.

339. *Poor Belgium*
Appetizers

> Nadar.
> Defeat of Janin.[73]
> The preface to J. Cæsar.
> The Lincoln case.

The people who treat Booth like a scoundrel are [worshipp] the same who adore Corday.

Is Lincoln a chastened rogue? The government of God is very complicated. The wicked is not necessary and divine; but as soon as it exists, God uses it to punish the wicked.

Always the sheep of Panurge. Journalists the worshippers of America & Belgium. — The will of Booth.

Booth is a brave man. I am glad that he died the death of the brave. — The surgeon. — Gendrin.

340. BRUSSELS
GENERAL CHARACTERISTICS
CONVERSATION

The Belgians' bizarre ideas about imperial tyranny. (The Emperor's boots full of mercury.)

They *believe* they are free because they have a Liberal Constitution.

They do not know how to be.
The Constitution (paper) & customs (life).

341. PARLIAMENTARY STYLE

[Press clipping from *Gazette Belge* (Nov. 30, 1865) detailing opposing views about patriotism, one being warlike, the other rational, each of which are expressed ironically, if not mockingly.]

342- PARLIAMENTARY STYLE

343. [Press clippings from *Gazette Belge* (Nov. 29, 1865) which, as the previous, demonstrate the ironic, mocking, snarky tone of the various politicians.]

344. PORTRAIT OF LÉOPOLD IST

[Press clipping from *La Publicité Belge* (Dec. 24, 1865) about the king's ability to feign all the characteristics of bourgeois royalty. It also speaks of his inflexible will, noting he had to believe until the last moment that a king dies only when he wants to.]

345. ENTRY OF NEW KING

[Press clipping from *La Publicité Belge* (December 24, 1865) depicting King Léopold II's entry into his capital. The article focuses on the king's demeanor (good looks, affable air, silky mustache, etc.) and his warm reception by the public, then describes how the population mourned the death of the previous king, its expressions of patriotic gaiety, and the new king's royal procession to the palace to the air of the Belle Hélène.][74]

346. *Death of the King*

[Press clipping from *L'Économie* (Dec. 24, 1865) outlining the contradictory stories written about the king. When clear he would soon be dead, he was asked if he wanted to see his children, to which he replied, "Nein, nein, nein." Moments later, he inquired into the ages at which different people died. Another account reports that the Duchess of Brabant questioned him about his seeing his children, to which he said, "There is no rush." Not hesitating, the Duchess brought the children to see him briefly. When the Duke of Brabant knelt beside his father and cried, the Duchess placed a crucifix before the King and asked him if he repented, to which he impatiently replied, "Yes, my dear, yes." Exhausted, the king closed his eyes; immediately thereafter, the Duchess placed the crucifix to his lips. The king lost consciousness and did not recover it. It was only then that his chaplain entered. The article ends with this declaration: "This is the real truth about the death of the King. I expose it to you sincerely, without comment, refraining from translating intentions, from assuming sentiments, from drawing convenient, risky, or unseemly inductions."]

347. BELGIAN LITERATURE

[Press clipping from *l'Étoile belge* (Dec. 24, 1865) about the death of Léopold II and how Mr. Havin had sent one of his editors to Brussels to give an account of all the details of the revolution, which could not fail before the advent of the King. On his arrival, the Frenchman would have leapt into a coach and ordered the driver to take him to the barricades. In reality, he came to Brussels to report on the funeral of the deceased king. As for Mr. d'Hormoys,[75] he claims to have been received by Léopold II so as to be decorated as a Belgian in thanks for his articles on the country. Since 1830, only one Belgian journalist has been so decorated! In the margins, CB writes: *Belgian jokes about the French (the Belgians pose for Happiness). Fury of the Belgians against Mr. d'Hormoys. The wretch was received by Léopold II.*]

348. Belgian literature flat on its belly
Biography of Léopold I by Victor Considérant
[Lengthy press clipping of 9 columns from *L'Indépendance belge* (Dec. 11, 1865) about the King. His career is described as the most nobly fulfilled, thereby one to serve as an example to all. He is deemed one of the most cultured princes of Europe, with a sharp intelligence and sagacity of judgment. When receiving an annual endowment of 50,000 books from the Estate of Claremont after his marriage, it is said that, with a scruple of disinterestedness and delicacy that cannot be praised too highly, he rescinded it as soon as he became King of the Belgians. Other details given include the death of his child, the marriage of his sister, his refusal of the Greek crown,

his accession to the Belgian throne, the nobility of his language and purity of his motives, the war with Holland and how the King's valor and military talents saved the honor of the Belgian flag, his obtaining concessions from former enemies and soothing national grudges, and his restoration of peace in constitutional ways, which saved Belgium from "the revolutionary contagion of 1848." Also noted are numerous occasions when unanimous agreement existed between the Crown & the people, including a moment in 1860 when French papers declared that only their own country counted as loyal and honest and that Belgium was ripe for annexation. To this, it is noted that every class was indignant. Further episodes are given, with the article ending by stating that Belgium will never forget Léopold I, who has earned the illustrious nickname of *Father of the Fatherland*.]

349. Little Buffooneries

(To be disseminated, each in its place.)

350. *Unclassified Documents*

>*Charabia* of Kertbeny (perhaps in the Beginning).[76]
>*Charabia* of St. Hubert (French Walloon).
>Regulations on prostitution (women & love).

The Ambiorix monument (art).[77]
A brochure about Boniface (politics, elections).
Biography of Mr. Kækebeck (elections).
A defamatory poster (elections).
The newspaper of equestrian statues (farcical journalism).
Official Holiday Program (entertainment).
Proudhon's letter on America.
Program of Veuillot.[78]
The Encyclical & the Syllabus.

351. [Title page in G. Vicaire's hand.]

352- ARGUMENT FOR THE BOOK ON BELGIUM
361.

Choice of titles:

The True Belgium.
Belgium Entirely Naked.
Belgium Stripped Bare.
A Capital for Laughter.
A Capital of Monkeys.

?

I. PRELIMINARIES

That he must, whatever Danton may say, always "carry his native land on the soles of his shoes."

France seems very barbarous, seen from up close. But go to Belgium and you will be less severe about your own country.

Just as Joubert thanked God for having made him a man and not a woman, you would thank God for not having made you a Belgian but a Frenchman.

Great merit of making a book on Belgium. To be entertaining while speaking of boredom, instructive while speaking of *nothing*.

To make a sketch of Belgium, there is, by [addition] <compensation>, an advantage that is made at the same time, a caricature of French stupidities.

Conspiracy of European flattery against Belgium. Belgium, in love with compliments, always takes them seriously.

How we sang the freedom, glory, and happiness of the United States of America among ourselves twenty years ago! Analogous stupidity regarding Belgium.

Why the French who lived in Belgium don't say the truth about this country. Because, as Frenchmen, they cannot confess that they were duped.

Voltaire's verses on Belgium.

2. BRUSSELS. Physiognomy of the Street

First Impressions. It's said that every city, every country, has its smell. Paris, it's said, smells, or *once smelled*, of acrid cabbage. Cape Town smells of sheep. There are tropical islands that smell of roses, musk, or coconut oil. Russia smells of leather. Lyon smells of coal. The Orient, in general, smells of musk and carrion. Brussels smells of black soap. The hotel rooms smell of black soap. The beds smell of [black] black soap. The napkins smell of black soap. The sidewalks smell of black soap. They wash facades and sidewalks, even when it rains. National, universal mania.

General *blandness* of life. Cigars, vegetables, flowers, fruit, cuisine, eyes, hair, everything *bland*, everything sad, tasteless, somnolent. The human physiognomy vague, somber, sleepy. Horrible fear, on the part of the Frenchman, of this *Soporific Contagion*.

The dogs alone are alive; they are the Negrœs of Belgium.

Brussels, much noisier than Paris; the reasons: the uneven pavement; the fragility & the sonority of the houses; the narrowness of the streets; the savage and immoderate accent of the people; the universal clumsiness: the *national whistle* (describe what it is), and the barking of dogs.

Few sidewalks, or sidewalks suddenly ending (consequence of individual freedom, pushed to the extreme). Terrible paving. No life in the street.

— Many Balconies, no one on the Balconies. *Spy mirrors*: a sign of boredom, curiosity, & inhospitality.

Sadness of a city without a river.

Nothing displayed in the shops. Flânerie, so dear to people gifted with imagination, impossible in Brussels. Nothing to see, and strolling impossible.

Innumerable lorgnettes. The reason. Remark of an optician. Amazing abundance of Hunchbacks.

The Belgian, or rather Brusselian face, obscure, shapeless, pale or vinous, strange construction of the jaws, menacing stupidity.

The gait of the Belgians, crazy and heavy. They look over their shoulders as they walk, continuously bumping into one another.

3. BRUSSELS
Life
Tobacco, cooking, wines

The question of Tobacco. Disadvantages of freedom.

The question of Cooking. No roasted meats. Everything is steamed. Everything is prepared with [rancid] rancid butter (due to economy, or taste). Execrable vegetables (either raw or with butter). No Stews. (Belgian cooks believe that very seasoned food is food doused with salt.)

The elimination of dessert and intermediate courses is symptomatic. No fruits (those from Tournai — are they good elsewhere? — are exported to England). They must therefore be imported from France or Algeria.

Finally, the bread is execrable, damp, soggy, burnt.

Alongside the *famous lie of Belgian liberty* and *Belgian cleanliness*, let us put *the lie of how cheap it is to live* in Belgium.

Everything is *four times* more expensive than in Paris, where only rent is expensive.

Here, everything is expensive, except the rent.

You can, if you have the strength, live as the Belgian. Description of the Belgian diet and hygiene.

— The question of wines. — Wine, curiosity & bric-a-brac object. Wonderful cellars, very rich, *all identical*. Expensive and heady wines. The Belgians *display* their wines. They do not drink them out of taste, but out of vanity, and as an act of *conformity*, so as to resemble the French.

— Belgium, a paradise for wine merchants. [There are] Drinks of the publicum: faro & juniper.

4. MORNINGS. WOMEN AND LOVE

No *women*, no *love*.

Why.

No gallantry in men, no modesty in women.

Modesty, a prohibited object, or an object that one doesn't feel the need for. General portrait of the Flemish, or at least of the Brabant woman. (Walloon woman, put aside, provisionally.)

General physiognomic type analogous to that of the sheep or the ram. — The smile, impossible, because of the recalcitrance of the muscles and the structure of the teeth and the jaws.

The complexion, in general, pallid, sometimes vinous. The hair, yellow. The legs, the breasts, enormous, [without] full of tallow. The feet, horror!!!

In general, a precociousness [monstrous corpu] from monstrous corpulence, marshy swelling, consequence of the moisture of the atmosphere and the piggishness of the women.

The stench of the women. Anecdotes.

Obscenity of Belgian ladies. Anecdotes about latrines *&* street corners.

As for love, refer to the indecency of the old Flemish painters. The sex of sixty-year olds. This people hasn't changed, and the Flemish painters remain relevant.

Here, there are *females*. There are no *women*.

— Belgian prostitution, high and low prostitution. Counterfeits of French vixens. French prostitution in Brussels.

— Extracts from the regulation on prostitution.

5. CUSTOMS (continued)

>Belgian coarseness (even among officers).
>Amenities of colleagues, among newspaper colleagues.
>Belgian criticism & journalism.
>Wounded Belgian vanity.
>Belgian vanity in Mexico.
>Baseness & servility.
>Belgian morality. Monstrosity in crime.
>Orphans & old men in adjudication.
>(The Flemish party, Victor Joly. His legitimate accusations against the spirit of apishness, — to put elsewhere, perhaps.)

6. CUSTOMS (continued)

>The Belgian Brain.
>Belgian Conversation.
>It is as difficult to define the Belgian character as it is to classify the Belgian in the rank of beings.
>He is an *ape*, but he is also a *mollusk*.
>A prodigious [versati] stupidity, an astonishing denseness. It is easy to oppress him, as history bears out; it is almost impossible to crush him.
>As we begin to judge, let us not deviate from certain ideas: Aping, Counterfeiting, Conformity,

Hateful Impotence, — we can classify all the facts under these different rubrics.

Their vices are counterfeit.

The Belgian *gandin*.

The Belgian patriot.

The Belgian slaughterer.

The Belgian free thinker, whose main characteristic is to *believe* that *you do not believe what you are saying*, since he cannot understand it. The counterfeiting of French impiety. Belgian obscenity, a counterfeiting of French dirty jokes.

Presumption *&* fatuity. — Familiarity. — Portrait of a Wallon dodo brain.

General *&* absolute horror of wit. Misfortunes of Mr. de Valbezen, French consul in Antwerp.

Horror of laughter. — Outbursts of laughter without cause. — A touching story is told; the Belgian bursts out laughing, to make the person believe that he has understood. — The Belgians are ruminants who digest nothing.

And yet, who would believe it? Belgium has its *Carpentras*, its *Bœotia*, of which Brussels jokes. Its Poperinghe.[79]

So there may be people who are more base than everyone I have seen.

7. MUSEUMS OF BRUSSELS

>Small town spirit. Jealousy. Calumny. Defamation. Nosiness about the affairs of others. Savoring the misfortune of others.
>
>Result of idleness *&* incompetence.

8. BRUSSELS: CUSTOMS

>Spirit of obedience *&* CONFORMITY.
>Spirit of association.
>Endless Societies (remains of the Guilds).
>In the individual, laziness of thought.
>In associating, individuals dispense with thinking individually.
>The Society of Pranksters.
>A Belgian would not believe himself happy if he did not see other people happy in the same way. So, he cannot be happy *of his own accord.*

9. BRUSSELS: CUSTOMS

>Spies.
>Belgian cordiality.
>Impoliteness.
>Belgian coarseness again. *The Gallic salt of the Belgians.*

The *pisser & the vomitter*, national statues that I find symbolic. — Scatological jokes.

10. BRUSSELS: CUSTOMS

Dimwittedness & laziness of the Belgians; in the man of the world, in businessmen, and in workmen.

Torpor & complication of bureaucracies.

The Post Office, the Telegraph Service, the Customs Warehouse.

Anecdotes about its bureaucracies.

11. BRUSSELS: CUSTOMS

Belgian morality. The merchants. Glorification of success. Money. — The story of a painter who wanted to deliver Jefferson Davis over in order to acquire an award.

Universal and reciprocal distrust, a sign of general immorality. Of any action, even a beautiful one, a Belgian doesn't assume a good motive.

Commercial improbability (anecdotes).

The Belgian is always inclined to rejoice at the misfortune of others. Besides, it's a motive for conversation — that's how bored they are!

General passion for Slander. I have been victimized several times.

General avarice. Great fortunes. No charity. It seems that there's a conspiracy to keep the publicum in misery & imbecility.

Everyone is a salesman, even the rich. Everyone is a dealer of goods.

Hatred of beauty, to counterbalance the *hatred of wit*.

Not being Conformist, that is the ultimate crime.

12. BRUSSELS: CUSTOMS

The myth of *Belgian cleanliness*. Of what it consists. — Clean things and dirty things in Belgium. Profitable trades: ceiling-bleachers. Bad trades: Bath Houses.

Poor neighborhoods. Popular customs. Nudity. Drunkenness. Begging.

13. BELGIAN ENTERTAINMENT

Grim & cold atmosphere.

Lugubrious silence.

Always the spirit of Conformity. They only have fun in groups.

The Vaux Hall.

The Casino.

The Théâtre de la Monnaie.

French vaudeville.

Mozart at the Théâtre du Cirque.

The Julius Langenbach troupe (no success because it had talent).

How I made a whole room applaud a ridiculous old dancer.

French vaudevilles.

Popular balls.

Ball games.

Archery contests.

The Carnival in Brussels. Drinks are never offered to one's dancing partner. Everyone jumps in place & in silence.

Barbarism of Children's games.

14. EDUCATION

Universities of the State, or of the Commune. Free universities. High schools.

No Latin, no Greek. Professional Studies. Hatred of poetry. Education to make engineers or bankers.

No metaphysics.

Positivism in Belgium. Mr. Hannon and Mr. Altmeyer, the one whom Proudhon called: *that old harpy!* His portrait. His style.

General hatred of literature.

15. THE FRENCH LANGUAGE IN BELGIUM

— Style of the few books written here.
— Some samples of the Belgian vocabulary.

They don't know French, *nobody* knows it, but everyone *affects* not knowing Flemish. It's good taste. The proof that they know it very well is that they *harangue* their servants in Flemish.

16. JOURNALISTS *&* LITTERATEURS

In general, here, the *litterateur* exercises another trade. Most often as an office worker.

Moreover, there is no literature. French, at least. One or two *chansonniers*, disgusting apes of Béranger's mischievousness. One Novelist, an imitator of the imitators of those Apes of Champfleury.[80] Savants, annalists, or chroniclers — that is, people who collect and others who buy stacks of paper at a low price (expense accounts of buildings *&* other things, inscriptions of princes, transcripts of the municipal councils, copies of archives) *&* then resell all of that as a history book.

Strictly speaking, everybody here is an annalist [or trad] (in Antwerp, everyone is a merchant of paintings; and in Brussels, there are also <rich> collectors who are curio dealers).

The Tone of Journalism. Numerous Examples. Ridiculous correspondence of the *Office of Publicity.* — *L'Indépendance belge.* — *L'Echo de parlement.* — *L'Étoile belge.* — *Le Journal de Bruxelles.* — *Le Bien public.* — *Le Sancho.* — *Le Grelot.* — *L'Espiègle.* — Etc., etc.

Literary Patriotism. A poster advertising a play.

17. BELGIAN IMPIETY. *An infamous chapter, that one! as well as the following:*

Insults [to] <against the> Pope. Impious propaganda. — Story of the death of the Archbishop of Paris (1848). — Representation of Pixerécourt's *Le Jésuite*, at the *Théâtre Lyrique*. — The Jesuit — puppet. — A procession. — Royal subscription for burials. — Campaign against a Catholic teacher. — About the Cemeteries Act. — Civil burials. — Disputed or stolen corpses. — A funeral for a *Solidarist*. — Civil burial of a woman. — Analysis of the rules of *free thought*. — Rules for Testaments. — A wager made by the Consumers of the Body of Our Lord!

18. IMPIETY & PRIEST-O-PHOBIA

Again, free thought! Again, the *Solidarists* and the *Freedmen!* Another rule for testaments: to steal a corpse from the Church. An article by Mr. Sauvestre, from *The L'Opinion nationale* on *free thought*. — Again still more stolen corpses. — Funeral of an abbot who died a *free thinker*. — Jesuit phobia. — What it is about *Our brave De Buck*, a former convict, persecuted by the Jesuits. — An assembly of Free Thought at my hotel, *The Grand Miroir*. — Belgian philosophical remarks. — Another burial of a *Solidarist* to the tune of: *"Ah! damn! so! Nadar's been afflicted!"*

The clerical party and the liberal party. Also beasts. — The famous Boniface, or Defré (a Belgian Paul-Louis Courier), is afraid of ghosts, digs up the corpses of children who died without the final sacrament in order to reinter them in holy ground, believes that he will die tragically, like Courier, and is accompanied in the evening so as not to be assassinated by the Jesuits. — My first interview with that fool. He was drunk. On his return from the garden, where he had gone to vomit, he interrupted the music to apostrophize in favor of *Progress &* against Rubens as a Catholic painter.

— The Abolishers of <the> Death Penalty, — very doubtless out of self-interest in the question, in Belgium as in France.

— Belgian impiety is a counterfeit of French impiety, but raised to the cubic power.

— The corner reserved for dogs or reprobates.

— Belgian Bigotry.

— The ugliness, villainy, wickedness, and stupidity of the Flemish clergy. — See Rops' lithograph of *the funeral*.

— The pious Belgians remind us of the cannibalistic Christians of South America.

— The only [perso] \<religious\> program that can be imposed on the *free thinkers* of Belgium is the program of Mr. de Caston, a French conjurer.

Curious opinion of a friend of Dumouriez on the parties in Belgium: "There are only two parties, the drunkards and the Catholics." — This country hasn't changed.

19. POLITICS

Electoral customs. Venality. The cost of an election in every locality is known. Electoral scandals.

Parliamentary practices. (Great number of examples of that.)

Belgian eloquence.

Grotesque discussion about electoral precautions.

The republican caucus. Counterfeiting of Jacobinism.

Belgium — always far behind the times.

20. POLITICS

Strictly speaking, there is no Belgian people. There are Flemish and Walloon races, and there are cities that are enemies of one another. Consider Antwerp. Belgium, the diplomatic harlequin.

Baroque history of the Brabant Revolution, undertaken against a philosopher King, and facing the French Revolution, a philosophical revolution.

A constitutional monarch is an automaton in a cheap inn. — Belgium is the victim of the electoral census. Why nobody here wants universal suffrage. The constitution is but a rag. Constitutions are *paper*. Customs are *everything*. — Belgian liberty is merely a word. — It's on paper, but it doesn't exist — it's *a park that no one has any need* of.

Comical situation of the House at some point. Two equal parties, minus *one* vote. — A magnificent electoral spectacle, as the French papers say.

Depiction of an electoral assembly. — Political speeches. Political eloquence. Pomposity. Disproportion between speech and object.

21. THE ANNEXATION

The annexation is a theme of Belgian conversation. It was the first word I heard here, two years ago. By dint of talking about it, they forced our [sheep]

<parrots> of French journalism to [occupy themselves with] <repeat the word>. — A large part of Belgium wants it. But that's an insufficient reason. France would have to consent to it. Belgium is a ragged, brutish child that leaps on the neck of a handsome gentleman & says to him: "Adopt me, be my father!" — the gentleman must consent though.

I am against annexation. There are <already> enough imbeciles in France, not to mention all of our old annexed places: the people of Bordeaux, the Alsatians, & others.

But I would not object to an invasion and a *Razzia*, in the ancient manner, in the manner of Attila. Everything beautiful can be brought to the *Louvre*. All this belongs to us far more legitimately than to Belgium, since they no longer understand it. — Besides, the Belgian ladies would make acquaintance with the Turcos, who aren't difficult to satisfy.

Belgium is a *shit-covered stick*; that especially is what creates its inviolability. *Don't touch Belgium!*

About the tyranny of the weak. Women and animals. That is what Belgian tyranny is constituted of in European opinion.

Belgium is guarded by a balance of rivalries. Yes, but if the rivals got along between themselves! In that case, what would happen?

(The rest, to be referred to in the epilogue, with conjectures on the future & advice to the French.)

22. THE ARMY

is more considerable, comparatively, than the other European armies; but it never makes war. Singular job of the budget!

This army, if entering war, would be ill adapted to march, on account of the conformation of the Belgian foot. But there are many men who could be trained very quickly.

All those beardless soldiers (enlistment is for a very short time) have the faces of children.

In that army, an officer can scarcely hope for advancement except by way of natural death or by the suicide of a superior officer.

There is great sadness among many young officers, who, moreover, have the knowledge and would make excellent soldiers, if the occasion occurs.

Rhetorical exercises at the military school, reports of imaginary battles, — sad consolations due to inactivity, for minds educated in the art of war.

More politeness in the army than in the rest of the nation. About that, nothing is surprising. Everywhere the sword honored, ennobled, and civilized.

23. KING LÉOPOLD I. HIS PORTRAIT.
ANECDOTES. HIS DEATH. MOURNING.

Léopold I, a wretched little German prince, has managed, as they say, *to make his bit of good-luck*. He did not leave in a carriage for exile. He came in sabots, he died rich, with more than a hundred million, in the midst of a European apotheosis. The final days, he was declared immortal. (Ridiculous panegyric. Léopold *&* Vapereau.)

A type of mediocrity, but cunning and with peasant perseverance, this Saxe-Cobourg cadet played everybody, *made his money*, and in the end stole the praises that are given only to herœs.

Opinion of Napoléon I on him.

His avarice, his rapacity. — His stupid ideas on etiquette taken from a German prince. His relationship with his family. — His pensions. The pension he received from Napoléon III.

Anecdote about the gardener.

His ideas about parks and gardens, which made them take him for a lover of *simple nature*, but which simply derived from his avarice.

The newspapers were falsified so that the King could not read anything alarming about his illness.

What is said behind me one morning by the Minister of the Interior. Ridiculous repugnance of the King for dying. — His disbelief about that subject. — He is chasing the doctors. — He runs to his mistress.

Invasion of the Duchess of Brabant and her children. She forcibly puts a crucifix to his mouth and asks if he is in any way repentant.

Traits of conformity between the death of the King and all dead Belgians. — His three chaplains are quarreling over his corpse. — Mr. Becker prevails *as he speaks French better!*

— The great Comedy of Mourning begins. — Black banners, panegyrics, apotheoses. — Drinking, pissing, vomiting of the whole population. — All the Belgians are in the street, [contained] noses in the air, contained and silent as at a masked ball. — They're having fun then. Never had Brussels, *in reality*, ever seen such a *party*. — It was [the fir] *its first* king who had just died. — The new King makes his entry to the air of *The Bearded King who Comes Forward (positive)*. — No one laughs. — There are some Belgians who sing: *Let us be soldiers*, a fine retort to those miserable *fransquillons* annexors.

24. FINE ARTS

In Belgium, no Art — Art has withdrawn from the country.

No artists, except Rops.

Composition, something unknown. Philosophy of those brutes, philosophy à la Courbet. To paint only what one sees (So *you* will not paint what *I* do not see). Specialists. — One painter for the sun, one for the moon, one for furniture, one for stuff, one for flowers, and subdivisions of specialties, to infinity, as in industry. — Collaboration becomes a necessary thing.

National taste for the ignoble. The old painters are therefore the true historians of the Flemish spirit. Here, the emphasis doesn't exclude stupidity, which explains the famous Rubens, a boor dressed in satin.

Of some modern painters, all pastichists, all of them, doubles of French talents. — The taste of amateurs. — Mr. Prosper Crabbe. The meanness of the famous interview with him. — How we make a collection. — The Belgians measure the value of artists by the price of their paintings. — A few pages on that infamous *charlatan* called Wiertz, a passion for English tourists. — Analysis of the Brussels Museum. Contrary to received opinion, the Rubens were much inferior to those in Paris.

Sculpture, nothing.

25. ARCHITECTURE, CHURCHES, WORSHIP

Civil and modern architecture. <Junk. Fragility of the houses.> No harmony. Architectural incongruities. — Good material. — Blue stone. Pastiches of the past. — In monuments, Counterfeits of France. — For the Churches, Counterfeiting the past.

The bygone. — The Gothic. — The 17th century.

— Description of the Grand Place of Brussels (very neat).

— In Belgium, always late, styles [are] linger and last longer.

— In praise of 17th-C. style, unknown style, and of which there are magnificent samples in Belgium.

— *Renaissance* in Belgium. — Transition. — Jesuit style. — [Style] Styles <of> the 17th century. — Rubens Style.

— The *Beguinage* Church in Brussels, *Saint-Pierre* in Malines, the *Jesuit Church* in Antwerp, *Saint-Loup* in Namur, etc., etc. …

— The Reaction of V. Hugo in favor of the beautiful Gothic night greatly damages our understanding of architecture. We have been too late. — Philosophy of the history of architecture, *according to me*. — Analogies with the corals, the *madrepores*, the formation of the continents, and finally with universal life. — Never gaps. — State of permanent transition.

— It can be said that the Rococo is [the last] [term] [term] (<the last bloom of the Gothic>).

— Cobergher, Faid'herbe, & Franquart.

— Opinion of Victor Joly on Cobergher, still derived from Victor Hugo.

— General wealth of churches. — A little boutique of curiosities, a bit of junk.

Description of this kind of [wealth] <wealth>.

Some churches either Gothic or 17th century.

Colored statues. Confessional, very decorated; — confessionals at Beguinage, Mechelen, Antwerp, Namur, etc. ...

— The Pulpits of Truth. — Very varied. — The real Flemish sculpture is made of wood, and it's mostly found in churches. — Sculpture not sculptural, not monumental; childish sculpture, <and jewels>. Sculpture of patience. —Besides, that art is dead like the others, even in Malines, where it has flowered so well.

— Description of some processions. Traces of the past, still subsisting in religious manners. — Great luxury. — Astonishing naiveté in the dramatization of religious ideas.

(To observe, in passing, the countless number of Belgian parties. There's always a celebration. Great sign of popular idleness.)

— Belgian devotion, stupid. — Superstition. The Christian God is not within reach of the Belgian Brain.

— The Clergy: heavy, coarse, cynical, lubricious, rapacious. In a word, it's Belgian. It was the Belgian who made the revolution of 1831, and he believes that all Belgian life belongs to him.

— Let us return a bit to the Jesuits & the Jesuit style. Style of genius. Ambiguous and complex character of that style. — (Vain and terrible.) — Great openings, <great bays,> great light — a mixture of figures, styles, ornaments, & symbols. — Some examples. <I saw a tiger's legs serving as windings.> In general, poor churches outside, except on the facade.

26. LANDSCAPE IN THE AREA AROUND BRUSSELS

Fatty, copious, damp, like the Flemish woman, — as gloomy as the Flemish man. — Very black greenery. — Climate wet, cold, hot, and humid: four seasons in one day. — Animal life hardly abundant. No insects, no birds. The animal <itself> flees from those cursed regions.

27. WALK TO MALINES

Malines is a good little hooded beguine. — Mechanical music in the air. — The Marseillaise carillon. — Every day resembles Sunday. — Crowd in the Churches. Grass in the streets. Old Spanish stench.

The Beguinage. Several Churches. — Saint-Rombaut. Notre-Dame. Saint Pierre. — Paintings of two Jesuit brothers on Missions. *Continuous* confessional. Wonderful symbol of the Pulpit, promising the Jesuits world domination, — unique sculpture that I saw. — Smell of wax and incense. — Rubens and Van Dyck. — Botanical Garden. Quick and clear stream. — Good wine from Moselle at Hôtel de la Levrette. — What a *Private Company* is.

28. WALK IN ANTWERP

[Phys] Meeting of the Archbishop of Mechelen. — Flat country. Black greenery. — New (!) and old fortifications, with English gardens. Finally, here is a city that has the air of a Capital! — The Place de Meir. The House of Rubens. The King's House. — Flemish *Renaissance*. City Hall. — The Church of the Jesuits, a masterpiece. — Still in the *Jesuitical style* (hodgepodge, chessboard, chandeliers, mystical and terrible Boudoir, mourning in marble, theatrical confessionals, theater and Boudoir, glory and transparency, angels and cupids, apotheoses and beatifications). — What I think of the famous Rubens, the closed churches, and the sacristans. — Cavalries *&* Madonnas. — Modern [vain] <pompous> style of some houses. — Majesty of Antwerp. Beauty of a great river. From there you have to see Antwerp. — The basins of Napoléon I. — Mr. Leys. — Plantin's printing house.[81] — The Rydeck dancehall, balls & prostitution. The Rydeck is a *joke*. It's like a large brothel from the Parisian suburbs.

Antwerpish customs, atrociously coarse. Funereal air of restaurant boys. — Antwerp politics (*will already be dealt with* in the chapter on *political customs*).

29. WALK TO NAMUR

We walk a bit in Namur. City neglected by travelers, naturally since the *directories* don't talk about it. — City of Vauban, Boileau, Van der Meulen, Bossuet, Fénelon, Jouvenet, Rigaud, Restout, etc. ... Memories of the *Lectern*. — *Saint-Loup*, the masterpiece of the masterpieces of the Jesuits. General impression. Some details. Jesuit architects, Jesuit painters, Jesuit sculptors, ornemannist Jesuits. — *The Recollects*. — Saint-Aubin, a small *Saint-Pierre* from Rome, in brick and blue stone outside, white inside, and with a convex portal. — Nicolai, false Rubens. — The street of blind finches. (The Duke of Brabant, now Léopold II, President of a Finch Academy.)

— Bizarre prostitution in Namur.

— Walloon population. — No more politeness.

— Portraits of Félicien Rops and his father-in-law, a severe magistrate, yet jovial, a great hunter, and a great quoter. He wrote a book on hunting and quoted me verses of Horace, verses from *The flowers of Evil*, and sentences of D'Aurevilly's. — Looked charming. — The only Belgian knowing Latin and knowing how to converse in French.

— I go to Luxembourg without knowing it.

— The landscape, black. The *Meuse*, steep & foggy.

— The wine of Namur.

30. HOLIDAYS IN LIÈGE

The Palace of the Princes-Bishops. — Cellars. Drunkenness. — Great pretensions to the French spirit.

31. WALK IN GHENT

Saint-Bavon, some beautiful things. Mausoleums. — Wild population. — Old town of revolting peasants, made a little separate group, and takes some airs of a Capital. Sad city.

32. WALK IN BRUGES

Phantom city, mummy city, pretty much preserved. It smells of death, the Middle Ages, Venice, black [spe], routine specters and tombs. — Great Beguinage; chimes. Some monuments. A work attributed to Michelangelo. However, Bruges is going, it also.

33. EPILOGUE. *The Future. Advice to the French.*

Belgium is what France would have become if it had remained under the hand of the Bourgeoisie. Belgium is lifeless, but not without corruption. — Cut into sections, divided, invaded, defeated, beaten, pillaged, the Belgian still vegetating, pure marvel of a mollusk. — *Noli me tangere*, a beautiful motto for her. Who would want to touch a *shit-covered stick?* — Belgium is a monster. Who would like to adopt it? Yet it has *several* elements of dissolution in it. The diplomatic harlequin can be dislocated from one moment to the next. — A part of it goes to Prussia, the Flemish part to Holland, and the Walloon provinces to France. — Great misfortune for us. — Portrait of the Wallon. — Ungovernable breeds, not because of excess vitality, but because of the total absence of ideas and feelings. It's nothingness. (Quote from Maturin and Dumouriez's friend.) — Commercial interests at stake, which I don't want to deal with. Antwerp wants to be a free city. — Once again, the question of annexation. — Small cities (Brussels, Geneva), wicked cities. Petty people, wicked people.

Tips to the French condemned to live in Belgium, so that they aren't robbed too much, insulted too much, or poisoned too much.

END

[DETACHED SHEETS]

[1] BRUSSELS

First impressions caused by the human face & gait.

Had I ever thought that one could be at once heavy & scatterbrained? The Belgians prove the laws of gravity by their gait. An object rushes by faster because it is heavier. They are, moreover, as uncertain as inanimate beings.

Threatening stupidity of faces. This universal stupidity worries us like an indefinite and permanent danger.

[2] BRUSSELS
GENERAL MUSEUMS
DANDYISM

Monkeys altogether.

Little sketch of the Belgian *gandin*. He proudly says: *I break it*, — or else: Gentlemen, *you do it for me with dough*. — If a woman who smells nice is close to him, not recognizing the [maternal] family scent, he will exclaim: *It's very stinky here!* then he suffocates with joy — he considers himself a Parisian, and looks with disdain at the Duke of Brabant, who smokes bourgeois cigars on two floors.

[3] *Poor Belgium*
General traits
Belgian morals

BELGIAN MORALITY

Verwee would like to win the 500,000 francs by delivering Jefferson Davis. Babou scandalized. "Lady! BECAUSE he is a scoundrel?" — Babou retorts: "If today you deliver a scoundrel for any sum, tomorrow you will deliver an honest man."

J. Leys, ashamed of his compatriot, tries to arrange things.

"You would deliver him by way of patriotism; *&* then you would commission a painting for the Washington Museum."

(Because there is a museum with a den of Yankees.)

"No," — said Verwee, who naively insists on infamy, — "I would first take the 500,000 francs, — and then I would perhaps consent [thereafter] to make a picture for the Museum."

Belgian morality.

[4] Little Belgian Amusements

Subscription list for victims of the Dour Catastrophe.

One Protestant *against* the Encyclical — 10 francs —, which presumably presupposes that it is [there is an identity between Charity] necessary to hate the pope for the same word, in what is charitable, and that the [same word in the same sentence] word *one* is a noun [sufficient].

[5] Fine Arts

The strongest, it is said, of the Belgian painters, the one whom those faro drinkers and those potato-eaters readily compare to Michelangelo, Mr. Alfred Stevens, usually paints a small woman (it's his tulip, always writing the same letter, receiving a letter, hiding a letter, receiving a bouquet, hiding a bouquet, in short, all the pretty nonsense that Deveria sold for 200 *sols*, without any greater pretension. — The great misfortune of this meticulous painter is, that the letter, the bouquet, the chair, the ring, the guipure, etc., become, in turn, the important object, the object that creates the eyes. — In short, he is a *perfectly* Flemish painter, insofar as there is perfection in *nothingness*, or in the *imitation of nature*, which is the same thing.

Tapestry
Jewelry

[6] MALINES

After visiting so many altars, chapels, and confessionals, a sensual traveler goes to Hôtel de la Levrette, not for dinner, great Gods! (for they do not dine in Belgium unless it's possible, without terror, to face the interminable *procession* of boiled *oxen*, roasted *sheep*, or so-called *calves*, *beefsteaks*, heads of calves, and cutlets for side dishes, and *hams* with salads for dessert) — but to drink a certain Moselle wine (firm, fine, dry, fresh, and clear) that left me with a vague memory of honey and musk. All that was lacking was [the taste of] some incense.

[7] *Poor Belgium*
EPILOGUE

Today, Monday, August 28, 1865, on a hot and humid evening, I wandered through the labyrinth of a street fair, a *Kermesse*, and in the streets named *Devil's Corner, Monks' Rampart, Our Lady of Sleep, Six Poker Chips*, & several others, with great delight I happened upon, suspended in the air, an abundance of signs of cholera. Have I invoked it sufficiently, that beloved monster? Have I studied well enough the advance signs of its arrival? How long is it, that horrible beloved of mine, that impartial Attila, that divine scourge whose victims are haphazard? Have I sufficiently begged the Lord My God to quicken its flight over the stinking banks of the *Senne*? And how I will delight in observing the death-throe grimaces of that hideous people entangled in the coils of its counterfeit-Styx, its *Briarious river*, which contains even more excrement than the sky above nourishes flies! — I shall delight, said I, in the terrors and tortures inflicted on that yellow-haired, naked, and lilac-colored race.

A beautiful observation: after many plaques dedicated to *union*, to *friendship*, to *fidelity*, to the *constitution*, to the Virgin Mary, I found one dedicated to: *the Police*.

Is it the English *policy*?

Inept people, in their joys and in their vows!

Read a book on Jesuit architecture, and a book on the political & educational role of the Jesuits in Flanders. —

Guides for Malines, Brussels, Namur, Liège, Ghent.

[8] BRUSSELS
Passim

To intertwine considerations on the customs of Belgians in French side dishes.

Nadar. Janin. Realism.
(Guiard);
The Punishment of Death, The Dogs.
The voluntary exiles;
The Life of Caesar (Dialogue of Lucian).

For these especially something very neat. Their revolting familiarity.

Lorikeet Fathers of Democracy.

The Coblentz.

Truths of Telemachus.

Old beasts, old Lapalisse.

[Good to] Specific to nothing, dodo brains.

Students of Béranger.

[We feel We fee]

Philosophy of pension masters *&* baccalaureate students.

I have never so well understood, on seeing it, the absolute stupidity of convictions.

Let us add that when we speak to them of revolution *for good*, they are terrified. *Old Rosières*. Me, when I consent to be Republican, *I do evil, consciously.*

Yes! *Long live the Revolution!*

Always! Everything the same!

But me, I'm not fooled! I've never been fooled! I say *Long live the Revolution!* as I would say: *Long live Destruction! Long live Expiration! Long live Punishment! Long live Death!*

Not only would I be happy to be a victim, but I would not hate to be an executioner — to feel the Revolution in two ways!

We all have the republican spirit in our veins, like the pox in our bones. We are Democratized & Syphilized.

[9] *Belgian Patriotism wounded*
Belgian self-esteem

> [Press clipping from *l'Etoile belge* (August 13, 1865). CB underlined this passage: "The speaker fenced with his hands & feet to prove that De Maistre is much greater than Voltaire." In the margins, in addition to the above two phrases, CB wrote this: *Nice sample of badinage, and especially good Belgian faith by an amateur litterateur and lawyer.*]

ENDNOTES

1. Amina Boschetti (1836–1881), a world-renowned Italian *prima ballerina assoluta*. French critics were in general critical of her because of her vivid miming, *tours de force*, and stockiness. See Baudelaire's poem on her, "On the Debut of Amina Boschetti," in *Les fleurs du Mal*.

2. Louis Joseph Defré (1814–1880), a Belgian lawyer and liberal representative of Brussels who advocated for the abolition of the death penalty. Writer of political and anticlerical pamphlets, Defré published his attacks under the pseudonym Joseph Boniface. In 1856, he became a member of the Masonic lodge *Les Amis Philanthropes*.

3. Roman pagan chthonic deities believed to represent the souls of deceased loved ones. Referred to as the *di inferi*, those who dwell below, as opposed to the *di superi*, the gods above.

4. Charles-François du Périer Dumouriez (1739–1823), a French general who won signal victories for the French Revolution in 1792–93. Following his invasion of Holland in late February of 1793, the Austrians defeated him. Concluding an armistice with the enemy, he sought to march on Paris and overthrow the National Convention, who then sent commissaries to relieve Dumouriez of his command. After deserting, his Girondin associates were discredited and the Jacobins had them expelled.

5. Armand-Joseph Guffroy (1742–1801), a lawyer and politician of the French Revolution. He voted in favor of the death of Louis XVI and against the reprieve. In 1794,

he denounced Joseph Lebon, the curé of the Constitutional Church in Pas-de-Calais and an associate of Robespierre's. In 1795 he was condemned to death as a terrorist.

6. See Voltaire's April 1, 1740 letter to A.M. De Formont, *Œuvres complètes de Voltaire*, Tome III (1827) 1086. Baudelaire quotes from the final verse but omits its last two lines.

7. Possibly a reference to François Béroalde de Verville (1556–1626), a French Renaissance poet, novelist, translator, and polymath. His *Le Moyen de parvenir* (1616?), a work often considered obscene but described by the author as *"une Satyre universelle,"* is a satire in the manner of Petronius and Rabelais. The book is rife with scatological comments.

8. French Romantic writer, mostly known for his *Rhapsodies* (1831), *Champavert* (1833), a book of 'immoral' Sadean tales, and *Madame Putiphar* (1839), a novel. Enid Starkie wrote a biography on him subtitled *The Lycanthrope* (1954), a figuration Borel used in *Champavert* to describe himself. Baudelaire referred to him as "one of the stars of the dark Romantic sky" and considered him a *"génie manqué."*

9. The passage hails from Charles Maturin's 1820 Gothic novel, *Melmoth the Wanderer*. What CB quotes continues in the original English: "and the sterility of nature itself is luxury compared to the sterility of human hearts, which communicate all the desolation they feel." The French translation splits the sentence in two.

10. French socialist songwriter and contemporary of Baudelaire's (born the same month and year, died 1870). The poet, who often heard Dupont sing, wrote a preface to his *Chants and Chansons* in 1851 & a second article in 1861 as part of his *Réflexions sur quelques-uns de mes contemporains*. See OC II, 26–36; 169–74.

11. Eugène Cormon (1810–1903), a French dramatist and librettist. He wrote for Bizet and Offenbach, among others. Verdi's *Don Carlos* is based in part on his play *Philippe II, Roi d'Espagne*. In 1927, Stanislavski staged Cormon's melodrama *The Gérard Sisters*. — Edouard Lassen (1830–1904), a Belgian-Danish composer and conductor. He conducted the first performance of Wagner's *Tristan und Isolde* in Weimar. Liszt expressed admiration for his music to Goethe's *Faust* (1876).

12. An elegant young man, more or less ridiculous, who frequented the boulevards during the Second Empire, obsessed as they were with appearance & with always being seen in the right places. The term was popularized via Paul Gandin, a character in Theodore Barriere's play, *Les parisiens* (1855), and linked etymologically to Boulevard de Gand (now Boulevard des Italiens), a meeting place for those who considered themselves elegant. Two other uses of the phrase: "Around, in the premier rows, parade the *gandin*" (Arthur Rimbaud, *Poesies*, 1870). "A surprising little world, brooding with pigs and imbeciles, who can be seen every day in Rue du Havre, properly dressed, with their *gandin* jackets, play rich and jaded men…" (Émile Zola, *La Curée*, 1871). The *gandin* for Baudelaire

is a negative figure, one he finds ridiculous, and so quite distinct from the dandy, a positive figure for Baudelaire.

13. A reference to the now forgotten writer and diplomat Eugène-Anatole de Valbezen (1815–1885), who wrote novels, plays, & reportage, including a book on India's colonization called *Les Anglais et L'Inde* (1857). Jules Verne drew much information from the book for his novel *The Steam House* (1880). Valbezen wrote articles under the pseudonym Major Fridolin. It is said that he was the son of Talleyrand. He was was Consul General in Antwerp in 1857.

14. Bœotia figured prominently in the rivalry between Athens and Sparta. The Bœotian League led an uprising against Sparta during the Corinthian War (395–387 BCE) but in the Battle of Chæronea (338) was thoroughly decimated in the struggle to preserve Greek independence from Macedonia. When Bœotia again challenged (335) Alexander the Great, it was destroyed; thereafter, it was of little consequence. — Poperinghe (today Poperinge) is a municipality located in the Belgian province of West Flanders. It once thrived as a cloth-making center. In 1382, French troops sacked and burned the town during the Hundred Years War. Under the Treaty of Nijmegen (1678), it passed into French Hands, then under the Treaty of Ryswick (1697), it passed to the Spaniards. In 1713, it was ceded to the Austrians under the Treaty of Utrecht, and in 1794 it was under French rule again. Subsequent to Napoléon's defeat, it became part of the United Kingdom of the Netherlands, from which Belgium revolted in 1830.

15. "That which pleases is twice repeated." Horace, *Ars poetica*.

16. The entire southern tip of the commune of Brussels from Notre Dame du Sablon onwards. The local culture and language particular to the period of Baudelaire's sojourn was destroyed long ago by regeneration projects that began in the late 19th C. In his 1987 work *Bruegel, or the Workshop of Dreams*, Claude-Henri Rocquet describes the Marolles as "a broken-down, deserted-looking quarter, forsaken by its former joy. It is not the slums, it is not the city. It is an out-of-the-way place, even though the center of Brussels, with its stores, old gold and noble house fronts, and its luxuries is only steps away and almost visible from deep inside these warrens. Perhaps old Marolles, the real one, still lives in the backrooms of the little bars." Laughably, a 2015 Berlitz guidebook says the area has never been gentrified.

17. "I am a man, nothing human is alien to me." Terence, *Heauton Timorumenos* (The Self-Tormentor) Act I.1.25.

18. "Woe to the vanquished."

19. Relatedly, in "Flares" §5, Baudelaire writes of friends having a secret desire to see a sick friend die so as to either verify his inferiority or to study an agony.

20. Reference to the "Société des Pinsonniers," a group based in Namur that would blind finches to make them sing better.

21. Hendrik van der Noot (1731–1827), a lawyer, nobleman, and founder of the conservative Statist party, whose headquarters he established in Breda when fleeing the Austrians. During the Disturbances of 1787, Van der Noot had been a champion of the Church and the noble classes. He wrote a pamphlet titled *Memoir on the Rights of the People of Brabant* (1787) and became a leader of the resistance movement. The Statist Party sought to gain Belgian independence by establishing a decentralized state based on ancient provincial constitutions.

22. A reference to Dupont's song "La vache blanche" which contains the lines: "I love my wife, ah! But I'd prefer / to see her die before my oxen do."

23. Jefferson Davis (1808–1889), American politician & President of the Confederate States from 1861–65.

24. *Queen Crinoline* refers to Hippolyte Cogniard and Ernest Blum's play *La Reine Crinoline, ou le Royaume des femmes: pièce fantastique en cinq actes et six tableaux*, which featured music by M.A.-D. Duvivier. — Epimenides (flourished 6th C. BCE?), Cretan seer, reputed author of religious and poetical writings, including a *Theogony*, *Cretica*, & other mystical works. Religious theories of an Orphic character were attributed to him as well. For his reputed claim — cited by St. Paul (Titus 1:12) — that all Cretans are liars, Epimenides, a Cretan, is credited with the invention of the paradox of the liar.

25. The original French word is "Essentançonner," which is Baudelaire's epenthesis of "*étançonner*," to prop up.

26. Pierre-Théodore Verhægen (1796–1862), a fiercely anticlerical Belgian lawyer and liberal politician who founded the Free University of Brussels. Verhaegen was a prominent member of the Brussels Free Masons lodge, too. He served as a deputy in the House of Representatives (1848–52; 1857–59).

27. A reference to Wilhelm von Kaulbach's painting, *Lotte Cutting Bread* (1862).

28. Late-Romantic Belgian painter Antoine Joseph Wiertz (1806–1865). Baudelaire lampoons him in his "Salon of 1859." Wiertz (as Baudelaire) is a subject of interest in Walter Benjamin's essay "Short History of Photography" and in his *Arcades Project*.

29. The correct Latin would be "*Pro refrigerio anime sue.*"

30. Louis-Eugène Cavaignac (1802–1857), a French general who suppressed the great revolt in Paris in 1848. He became known as "the butcher of June." Although deemed Chief Executive of France, he lost the presidential election to Louis-Napoléon.

31. "<u>Sues</u> *eum non cognoverunt.*" This is a passage from Job (2:12), but the original reads: "*Cumque elevassent procul oculos suos, non cognoverunt eum, et exclamantes ploraverunt, scissisque vestibus, sparserunt pulverem super caput suum in caelum.*" In writing "*Sues eum non cognoverunt,*" the Belgians have both the syntax and spelling incorrect. The underlining is Baudelaire's.

32. Pierre-Jean de Béranger (1780–1857), French poet and writer of popular songs and satires, celebrated for his liberal and humanitarian views. Robert Louis Stevenson wrote a biography on him for *Encyclopaedia Britannica*.

33. *Gougnotte* is argotic French for lesbian, variously defined at the time (as at least two dictionaries attest) as either a woman who hates men and has unusual morals, or a person devoted to the vice that lesbians made famous. In 1864, the year Baudelaire met Félicien Rops, Rops made a frontispiece to Henri Monnier's book *Deux gougnottes: Dialogues infâmes*, which was published by Poulet-Malassis, Baudelaire's publisher. — *Lupanar* (Latin for prostitute, or she-wolf) is the famous brothel in Pompeii.

34. *Rara avis in terris nigroque simillima cygno* ("A bird as rare upon the earth as a black swan"). Juvenal, *Satires*, 6.165.

35. The underlining is CB's emphasis.

36. René-Charles Guilbert de Pixerécourt (1773–1844), a French theater director and playwright. The play Baudelaire refers to here & later (§§171, 172, and §17 of 352–61), *Le Jésuite*, was co-written with V. Ducange.

37. The correct Latin phrase is: *Quem deus vult perdere, prius dementat*. It is an ancient Greek proverb adapted from Publius Syrus: *Those whom the gods would destroy, they first make mad*. Commonly quoted, the proverb is found in Sophocles, Euripides, Byron, etc.

38. Dechamps was a journalist, the leader of a section of Montalembertian Belgian Catholics, and a cabinet member. He gave speeches on education and communal organization. In 1864, during the ministerial crisis, he submitted to the king a program that sought to: 1) diffuse fractions between liberals and clericals; 2) lower the provincial and communal franchise and increase the power of the clergy and the aristocracy; 3) decentralize; and 4) propose general changes that would lend greater popularity to his party.

39. "Free examination" refers to *le libre examen*, a principle that advocates freedom of judgment and the rejection of authority in matters of knowledge. It is based on Aristotle's thought and was the founding principle of the universities of the Middle Ages.

40. *Affranchis*: a former French legal term denoting a freedman or emancipated slave, used to refer pejoratively to mulattœs.

41. Charles Sauvestre (1818–1883), a militant anticlerical journalist and writer. Founder of the *Revue Moderne* and author of *Le Clergé et l'éducation, question urgente, Le parti dévot*, and *Monita secreta Societatis Jesu*, amongst others.

42. Benedict Franz de Buck was accused of threatening to kill Lhoire, a Belgian Jesuit. De Buck's trial was held from May 13–16, 1864. He was exonerated and the Jesuits Lhoire, Hessels, Bossaert, and Franqueville were convicted of inducing the millionaire, William de Boey, to make a will handing over his estate of millions to the Belgian Jesuits,

unjustly superseding De Boey's poor relatives, the De Bucks, and appointing a sham heir, the lawyer Valentyns, who had relations with the Jesuits but who was entirely unknown to De Boey. De Buck uttered his threat when in a rage at learning of his disinheritance as engineered by the Jesuits.

43. Paul-Louis Courier (1772–1825), a French classical scholar and pamphleteer esteemed for his brilliant style and antimonarchist writings. Courier translated from Latin and Greek and discovered an unknown fragmentary manuscript of the Greek writer Longinus in a Florentine library. Under the Restoration, he settled in France and published pamphlets defending the rights of the peasants and attacking reactionary politicians and the clergy. Courier was murdered by a servant he dismissed for having an affair with his 19-year-old wife.

44. The pseudonym of Toulouse-born mathematician Léon-François-Antoine Aurifeuille (1822–1882). Under his pseudonym, Aurifeuille wrote books on card games, miracles, and superstition.

45. The Shabako Stone, which hails from Memphis, Egypt, is said to be of great importance in understanding man's evolution from polytheism to monotheism. For a brief overview of the history of the stone and how it has been interpreted, see Simson R. Najovits' *Egypt, Trunk of the Tree, Vol. I: A Modern Survey of an Ancient Land* (2003) 107–112, 178.

46. The Ursulines were religious institutes of the Catholic Church, the most prominent being the one founded by St. Angela Merici (1470–1540) at Brescia in 1535. It was formed to nurse the sick and educate girls.

47. Carlo Armellini (1777–1863), an Italian statesman whom Pope Pius made a Consistorial Advocate at the Papal Court. In 1848, Armellini joined the Anti-Papals, then became Minister of the Interior. He died in Saint-Jostten-Noode in 1863.

48. A pagan dance performed around eggs, sometimes called the hop dance or hop-egg. In "The Knight's Tale," Chaucer refers to its performers as *"hoppesteres."* For a lengthier description, and accompanying piece of music, see Grace T.H. Kimmins' *The Guild of Play Book of Festival and Dance*, Vol. 2 (1909) 26–27.

49. Different from a café, an *estaminet* is a type of local pub featuring not only poetry and song, but games, too. *Estaminets* are of particular note for their welcoming women and children, hence quite different from bohemian cafés.

50. This slang refrain was supposedly coined by Baudelaire & occurs several times in this book.

51. Pierre Clément Eugène Pelletan (1813–1884), a French writer, journalist, & politician. He moved to Paris in 1833 and was close to George Sand and Lamartine. While a free thinker, he was also a Deist and a spiritualist. As Condorcet, he believed in indefinite & continuous progress.

A fierce opponent of Napoléon III, he joined the opposition to the regime of the Second Empire. He was a Republican Deputy of the Seine from 1863–1870. In 1864, he was initiated a Freemason.

52. Alfred Cadart (1828–1875), a publisher and amateur etcher who had a significant impact on the revival and sale of etchings in France and elsewhere. In 1862, he founded the *Société des Aquafortistes* and, in collaboration with master printer Auguste Delâtre, served as its director. Like Baudelaire, Cadart was critical of photography, which he dismissed as mechanical and uninspired, whereas etching was "the caprice, the fantasy, the most immediate way to convey one's thoughts." In 1866, he founded the French Etching Club of New York. The Rops painting Baudelaire refers to was made in 1863.

53. An 1863 meeting of Belgian Catholic leaders held in the city of Malines. The congress helped create the first Catholic political organization in continental Europe. Initiated by Cardinal Sterkyx, the archbishop of Malines, it was a landmark in the development of church-state relations. Sterkyx sought to combat the anticlericalism of liberals, who had gained control (via elections) of the Belgian government in 1857. The Catholics defended the church by claiming to defend the constitution.

54. A possible veiled reference to Victor Hugo, who practiced table turning with his sons. When Mme. de Girardin, an apostle of spiritism, introduced the practice to Hugo, he first found it puerile; later, when a manifesting spirit claimed to be his recently deceased daughter, Léopoldine,

he became a devotee of the practice. Another entity to supposedly have manifested at the séances was Aeschylus, who expressed himself in French verse in Hugo's style. And on January 13, 1854, none other than Shakespeare himself visited Hugo. When the Bard was asked what he did on April 23, 1606, he said he kissed Corneille, who had been born just then. Hugo corrected him and said, "No, I said 1606, not 1616. Collect your thoughts and consider whether that day Shakespeare did not meet another great representative of human thought." The reply was no. During another séance, after Shakespeare declared that he would recite a poem, Hugo asked if he would do so in English or in French, to which the Bard replied, "The English language is inferior to the French." Hugo's son, François-Victor, believed that the soul of Shakespeare had taken possession of him and aided his translations of the Bard into French, presumably of course improving upon the originals. For one study of this material, see John Chambers, *Victor Hugo's Conversations with the Spirit World: A Literary Genius's Hidden Life* (1998; 2008).

55. Jean-François Vleminckx (1800–1876) was head of the Civil Guard Health Service, then Inspector General of Army Health Services. In that capacity, he fought against epidemics from typhus to dysentery, cholera, etc. From 1848–1864, he was the provincial councilor for Brabant. In 1864, he was elected Liberal Representative of the district of Brussels, a position he held until 1876. His main concern was with hygiene among the working class and the restrictive regulation of women's and child labor in coalmines. He is the co-author of *Essai sur l'ophtalmie des Pays-Bas* (1825).

56. A possible reference to Coomans' questioning the minister of war about Belgian soldiers receiving authorization from the government to participate in military service in Mexico, an inquiry that prompted intense debate. The motion of Coomans, who expressed regret over the governmental authorization of serving in a foreign country, failed by a vote of 39 for and 53 against. For further details, see *House Documents, Otherwise Publ. as Executive Documents*, Vols 1–15 (1865).

57. Native Algerian *tirailleurs* (infantry soldiers) in the French army, dressed as Turks. Louis Faid'herbe created the Senegalese *Tirailleurs* when governor there. See more on Faid'herbe below.

58. Victor Prosper Considérant (1808–1893), a French utopian Socialist and disciple of Fourier. Following the 1848 revolution, Considérant was elected to the Constituent Assembly. A year later, he had to flee France due to his political activity. Considérant settled in Brussels for two decades then returned to Paris in 1869. He is the author of *Destinée sociale, Manifeste de la démocratie au XIXe siècle, Principes du socialisme*, & many other works. When visiting the US, he founded a communist colony, La Réunion.

59. *Fransquillons*: strong term of abuse used by Dutch-speaking Flemings for Gallicized Flemings.

60. Belgian photographer Charles Neyt (1833–1908), who in 1864 took one of the last great portraits of Baudelaire.

61. Louis Gustave Vapereau (1810–1906), a man of letters, lexicographer, philosophy professor, and lawyer. He is most well known for his *Dictionnaire universel des contemporains* (1858). Vapereau also wrote studies on the penal colony of Mettray, penitentiary reform, free thought, and contributed to the *Dictionnaire des sciences philosophiques*.

62. Jacques Emmanuel Prosper Crabbe (1827–1889), a Belgian senator and agent of the Brussels Stock Exchange. As a financial reporter, he wrote for publications such as *Le Journal de Bruxelles*, *L'Indépendance belge*, and *L'Étoile belge*. He had an impressive collection of paintings, including works by old masters (Rembrandt, Rubens, Hals, Van Ostade, Teniers, etc.) and those contemporary to his time (Corot, Delacroix, Gericault, Millet, et cetera). — Jules Van Præt (1806–1887) was a Belgian diplomat and personal secretary of King Léopold I. Author of *Essais sur l'histoire politique des derniers siècles*. Described by some as an ardent royalist and cold patriot.

63. Wenceslas Cobergher (1560–1634), a Flemish Renaissance architect, engineer, painter, antiquarian, etc. Some of his works include the basilica of Scherpenheuvel in Brabant, which took 15 years to build. He also designed the town hall of Ath, Hainaut, the church of St. Augustine, Antwerp, and the St. Hubertus Chapel, Tervuren. — Louis Faid'herbe (1818–1889), governor of French Senegal (1854–61; 1863–65) and principle founder of France's colonial empire in Africa. He established Dakar, French West Africa's future capital, and was an early opponent of militant Islamicism. — Jacob Franquart (1582/83–1651), a

Flemish painter, court architect, and copper plate engraver. He designed the Temple des Augustins (1642), which was destroyed in 1893.

64. Pen name of French educator, translator, and author Hippolyte Léon Denizard Rivail (1804–1869). Founder of Spiritism, he wrote books on arithmetic, education, and most famously, the five volume *Spiritist Codification*.

65. Possible reference to *Suspiria de Profundis* and the three goddesses of sorrow, Our Ladies of Sorrow (Notre-Dame des Tristesses): Mater Lacrymarum, Mater Suspiriorum, and Mater Tenebrarum. De Quincey referred to them as the "*Semnai Theai*, or Sublime Goddesses, these were the *Eumenides*, or Gracious Ladies … of my Oxford dreams." Baudelaire translated De Quincey's *Confessions…* and *Suspiria…* as *Un mangeur d'opium*. For an exceptional study of Baudelaire's translation practices, see Emily Salines, *Alchemy and Amalgam* (2004).

66. Edmond-Désiré Couty de la Pommerais (1836–1864), a homeopathic doctor practicing in Paris. To acquire financial gain, he murdered his mother-in-law, and later his former mistress, Séraphine de Pauw, by poisoning them with digitalin. He was convicted only of the second murder and guillotined for it on June 9, 1864. For details on Pommerais' dastardly scheme and the ingenious methods undertaken to prove his crime, see Linda Stratmann's *The Secret Poisoner* (2016) 204–08, 260, 304 footnotes 6 and 9.

67. Founded in Berlin by Albert Hofmann and David Kalisch, *Kladderadatsch* was first published on May 7, 1848.

Critical of the German government and hostile to socialism when it was first established, the journal originally favored moderate reform. Circulation rose from 22,000 in 1858 to 50,000 in 1872. Its politics changed over time and it grew less satirical and more conservative. In 1923, the journal would praise Hitler for his patriotic spirit.

68. Belgian painter Alfred Jacques Verwee (1838–1895).

69. Esteemed doctor Augustin-Nicolas Gendrin (1796–1890). He is the author of *Mémoire médico-légal* and many other works.

70. Károly Mária Kertbeny (1824–1882), Austrian-born Hungarian journalist, memoirist, and human rights campaigner. He translated Petőfi, Arany, and Jókai into German & was friends with Heinrich Heine, George Sand, Alfred de Musset, Hans Christian Andersen, and the Brothers Grimm. He coined the terms heterosexual and homosexual and argued that the Prussian sodomy law violated the rights of man.

71. Probable reference to the Gœthals Collection, Antwerp.

72. Probable reference to the Coûteaux-Vauthier Documents housed in the Jaarbœk van het Koninklijk Museum, Antwerp.

73. Jules Gabriel Janin (1804–1874), esteemed French theater critic, novelist, and literary historian known for his mercurial points of view. He wrote for *Figaro*, *Quotidienne*, and *Journal des Débats*. The *American Literary Gazette*

commences its continental correspondence by stating that "the public conscience has been revolted by the defeat of Mr. Jules Janin" (June 15, 1865) 70. This refers to Janin's seeking to obtain the seat formerly occupied by Duke Pasquier in the Académie Française. He lost to Dufaure, an eminent lawyer.

74. An opera *bouffe* in three acts by Jacques Offenbach with an original French libretto by Henri Meilhac and Ludovic Halévy. First performed at Théâtre des Variétés in Paris on December 17, 1864.

75. Paul d'Hormoys (1829–1889), author of *Sapajou. Histoire d'une Abonné l'Opéra*, and *L'Empire de Soulouque*.

76. *Charabia* is colloquial French for double Dutch, or a word meaning gibberish. It is also applied as an ethnic slur to the Auvergnats.

77. Ambiorix (Gaulish for "king in all directions") was, together with Cativolcus, prince of the Eburones, leader of a Belgic tribe of northeastern Gaul (Gallia Belgica), where modern Belgium is located. In the 19th C., Ambiorix became a Belgian national hero because of his resistance against Julius Cæsar. See Caesar's *Commentarii de Bello Gallico*.

78. Louis Veuillot (1813–1883), French journalist and author who participated in the popularization of ultramontanism, a philosophy that favored papal supremacy. Veuillot's excoriating critiques of America *&* its technocratic culture are ones Baudelaire would have concurred with.

To Veuillot, America was barbaric, profligate, bankrupt, tyrannical, if not genocidal (he refers to the systematic destruction of Native Americans in one diatribe), and a slave to machinery. A representative passage of his views: "America might founder in the ocean once and for all, and the human race would suffer no loss thereby. ... Thus far, there is no civilization in America, and as far as appearances go, there never will be" (*L'Univers*).

79. Carpentras is a commune in the Vaucluse department in the Provence-Alpes-Côte d'Azur region in southeastern France. It stands on the banks of the Auzon.

80. Pseudonym of Jules-François-Félix Husson (1821–1889), French novelist and journalist and friend of Baudelaire's. Theoretician of the Realist movement, Champfleury was also an early champion of both Courbet and El Greco. The January 1848 issue of *Le Corsaire-Satan* contains Baudelaire's review of some of Champfleury's work. In 1865, Champfleury published two books on caricature, *Histoire de la caricature* and *Histoire de la caricature moderne*. The latter adopts much of Baudelaire's own views on caricature.

81. Printing plant and publishing house dating from the Renaissance & Baroque periods. Now the Plantin-Moretus Museum, it contains printing equipment from the time, a library and archive, and art works, including a painting by Rubens. Its archives were added to UNESCO's Memory of the World Register. Christophe Plantin (1520–1589) was the greatest printer-publisher of the second half of the 16th C. Jan Moretus was his assistant, business manager, & eventual successor.

APPENDIX

April 14, 1864

To the Editor in Chief of *Figaro*

Sir,

It's happened to me more than once that I've read *Figaro* & felt scandalized by the uninhibited plundering which, unfortunately, forms a part of the talent of your collaborators. To be honest, that kind of "insurrectionist" literature that we call the "little newspaper" is not very entertaining for me and almost always shocks my instincts of justice and modesty. However, whenever a great stupidity, a monstrous hypocrisy, one of those that our century produces with inexhaustible abundance stands before me, I immediately understand the usefulness of the "little newspaper." Thus, you see, I give myself over to near harm, with good grace.

That's why I thought it appropriate to denounce one of those outrageous remarks, one of those absurdities, before it makes its final explosion.

April 23 is the date when Finland itself is said to celebrate the three-hundred-year anniversary of Shakespeare's birth. I do not know if Finland has any mysterious interest in celebrating a poet who is not native born, if she has the desire to make some malicious toast about the English poet-comedian.

APPENDIX

I understand, strictly speaking, that the *litterateurs* of Europe as a whole wish to join together in a common outpouring of admiration for a poet whose grandeur (like that of several other great poets) makes him cosmopolitan; however, we might note in passing that, while it is reasonable to celebrate poets from all countries, it would be even more accurate for everyone to celebrate, first of all, his own. Every religion has its saints, and I note with difficulty that so far there has been little concern here to celebrate the anniversary of the birth of Chateaubriand or Balzac. Their glory, I will say, is still too young. But that of Rabelais?

Thus that is something accepted. We suppose that, driven by spontaneous recognition, all the *litterateurs* of Europe want to honor the memory of Shakespeare with perfect candor.

But are the Parisian *litterateurs* driven by such a disinterested feeling, or rather obey, without their knowledge, a very small coterie that pursues a personal and particular goal, very distinct from the glory of Shakespeare?

I have been, on this subject, the confidant of some jokes and complaints that I wish to share with you.

A meeting was held somewhere, no matter where. Mr. Guizot was to be part of the committee. No doubt they wanted to honor him as the signatory of a poor translation of Shakespeare. The name of Mr.

Villemain was also registered. In the past, he spoke, as best he could, of English theater. It's a sufficient pretext, though that soulless mandrake, to tell the truth, is destined to make a strange figure before the statue of the most passionate poet in the world.

I do not know if the name of Philarète Chasles, who has contributed so much to popularize English literature, had been registered; I doubt it very much, and I have good reasons for that. Here, at Versailles, a few steps away from me, lives an old poet who has made a mark, not without honor, in the romantic literary movement; I mean Mr. Emile Deschamps, translator of *Romeo and Juliet*. Eh well! sir, would you believe that name did not pass without some objections? If I asked you to imagine why, you would never guess. Deschamps was for a long time one of the main employees of the Ministry of Finance. It is true that he has for a long time also been retired. But, in fact, justice, gentlemen, the factotums of democratic literature, do not look so closely at it, and that crowd of little young men is so busy doing their business that Justice learns with astonishment that such an old fellow, to whom she owes a lot, is not yet dead. You will not be surprised to learn that Mr. Théophile Gautier was almost excluded as a spy. (Spy is a term that means an author who writes articles on drama and painting in the official state paper.) I am not at all surprised, nor you probably, that the name of Mr.

Philoxène Boyer has raised many recriminations. Mr. Boyer is a beautiful spirit, a very beautiful spirit, in the best sense. His is a flexible and great imagination, and he is a very erudite writer, who has, in time, commented on Shakespeare's works in brilliant improvisations. All that is true, incontestable; but unfortunately! the unfortunate man has given some signs of a rather lively monarchical lyricism. In that he was sincere, no doubt; but whatever! such unfortunate odes in the eyes of those gentlemen annulled all his merit as a Shakespeareanist. Relative to Auguste Barbier, translator of *Julius Caesar*, and to Berlioz, author of a *Romeo and Juliet*, I do not know anything. Mr. Charles Baudelaire, whose taste for Saxon literature is well known, had been forgotten. Eugène Delacroix is very happy to be dead. No doubt he would have been shut out of the gates of the feast, he, a translator in his style of *Hamlet*, but also the corrupt member of the Municipal Council; he, the aristocratic genius, who was acting cowardly so as to be polite, even to his enemies. On the other hand, we will see the Democrat Biéville toast, *with restrictions*, the immortality of the author of *Macbeth*, and the delicious Legouvé, and Saint-Marc Girardin, that hideous courtier of mediocre youth, and the other Girardin, the inventor of the Escargotic Compass and the subscription of one *sou* per head for the abolition of the war!

But, the height of the grotesque, the *ultimate* of ridicule, the irrefutable symptom of the hypocrisy of the demonstration, is the appointment of Mr. Jules Favre, as a member of the Committee. Jules Favre and Shakespeare! Do you understand that outrage? Doubtless, Mr. Jules Favre is a mind sufficiently cultivated to understand the beauties of Shakespeare, and, as such, he may come; but if he has two *liards* of common sense, and if he does not want to compromise the old poet, he has only to renounce the absurd honor conferred upon him. Favre in a Shakespearean committee! That is more grotesque than a Dufaure at the Academy!

But, in truth, the organizers of the *little* party have much more to do than to glorify poetry. Two poets, who were present at the first meeting of which I spoke to you a moment ago, remarked sometimes that one forgot this one or that one, sometimes that one would have to do this or that; and their observations were made only in the literary sense; but each time, one of the little humanitarians answered them: "You do not understand *what it is*."

No ridicule will fail at this solemnity. It will also be natural to celebrate Shakespeare at the theater. When it comes to a representation in honor of Racine, we play, after the ode of circumstance, the *Pleaders* and *Britannicus*; if it's Corneille that is celebrated, it will be the *Liar* and the *Cid*; if it's Molière,

The Penguin and *The Misanthrope*. Now, the director of a great theater, a man of gentleness and moderation, an impartial courtier of goat and of cabbage, said recently to the poet in charge of composing something in honor of the tragic Brit: "Try to slip in there the praise of French classics, and then, to better honor Shakespeare, we will play. *We must swear by nothing!*" That is a little proverb by Alfred de Musset.

Let's talk about the true purpose of that great jubilee. You know, sir, that in 1848 an adulterous alliance was made between the literary school of 1830 and democracy, a monstrous and bizarre alliance. Olympio renounced the famous doctrine of *art for art's sake*, and since then, he, his family and his disciples, have not ceased to preach to the people, to speak for the people, and to show themselves on every occasion their friends and the regular patrons of the people. "Tender and deep love for the people!" From then on, all that they can love in literature has taken revolutionary and philanthropic color. Shakespeare is a socialist. He never suspected it, but it does not matter. A kind of paradoxical criticism has already tried to disguise the monarchist Balzac, the man of the throne and the altar, as a man of subversion and demolition. We are familiar with that kind of trickery. Now, sir, you know that we are in a time of honoring, and that there is a class of men whose throats are clogged with toasts, speeches, and unexpressed cries, which, very naturally, seek investment. I have known people who have been paying close attention to mortality, especially among celebrities, and actively seek among families and in cemeteries to praise the dead that they had never known. I point out to you Mr. Victor Cousin as the prince of the genre.

Every banquet, every festival, is a good occasion to give satisfaction to such French verbiage; orators are the least lacking fund; and the little coterie of that poet (in whom God, by a spirit of impenetrable mystification, amalgamated foolishness with genius), judged that the moment was opportune to use that indomitable mania for the benefit of the following purposes, to which the birth of Shakespeare will serve only as a pretext:

1. To prepare and incite the success of V. Hugo's book on Shakespeare, a book which, like all his books, is full of beauties and stupidities, will perhaps still vex his most sincere admirers;

2. Toast to Denmark. The question is exciting, and we owe it to Hamlet, who is the most famous prince of Denmark. It will be better in the situation than the toast to Poland, which I am told was offered at a banquet given to Mr. Daumier.

Then, according to the occurrences and the particular *crescendo* of stupidity among the crowds gathered in one place, to make toasts to Jean Valjean, to the abolition of the death penalty, to the abolition of misery, to *Universal Fraternity*, to the diffusion of enlightenment, to the *true* Jesus Christ, *the legislator of Christians*, as they used to say, to Mr. Renan, to Mr. Havin, etc., and finally to all the stupidities peculiar to this 19th C., in which we have the wearisome happiness of living, and where everyone is, it seems, deprived of the natural right *to choose his brothers*.

Sir, I forgot to tell you that women were excluded from the party. Beautiful shoulders, handsome arms, handsome faces, and shining demeanors could have hurt the democratic austerity of such solemnity. However, I think we could invite some actresses, if only to give them the idea of playing a little Shakespeare and competing with the Smiths & the Faucites.

Keep my signature, if you wish; delete it, if you think it does not have enough value.

Please accept, Sir, the assurance of my distinguished feelings.

COLOPHON

BELGIUM STRIPPED BARE

was handset in InDesign CC.

The text & page numbers are set in *Adobe Garamond Premiere*.
The titles are set in *Quasimoda*.

Book design & typesetting: Alessandro Segalini
Cover design: István Orosz & CMP

BELGIUM STRIPPED BARE

is published by Contra Mundum Press.
Its printer has received Chain of Custody certification from:
The Forest Stewardship Council,
The Programme for the Endorsement of Forest Certification,
& The Sustainable Forestry Initiative.

Contra Mundum Press   New York · London · Melbourne

CONTRA MUNDUM PRESS

Dedicated to the value & the indispensable importance of the individual voice, to works that test the boundaries of thought & experience.

The primary aim of Contra Mundum is to publish translations of writers who in their use of form and style are *à rebours*, or who deviate significantly from more programmatic & spurious forms of experimentation. Such writing attests to the volatile nature of modernism. Our preference is for works that have not yet been translated into English, are out of print, or are poorly translated, for writers whose thinking & æsthetics are in opposition to timely or mainstream currents of thought, value systems, or moralities. We also reprint obscure and out-of-print works we consider significant but which have been forgotten, neglected, or overshadowed.

There are many works of fundamental significance to *Weltliteratur* (& *Weltkultur*) that still remain in relative oblivion, works that alter and disrupt standard circuits of thought — these warrant being encountered by the world at large. It is our aim to render them more visible.

For the complete list of forthcoming publications, please visit our website. To be added to our mailing list, send your name and email address to: info@contramundum.net

Contra Mundum Press
P.O. Box 1326
New York, NY 10276
USA

OTHER CONTRA MUNDUM PRESS TITLES

Gilgamesh
Ghérasim Luca, *Self-Shadowing Prey*
Rainer J. Hanshe, *The Abdication*
Walter Jackson Bate, *Negative Capability*
Miklós Szentkuthy, *Marginalia on Casanova*
Fernando Pessoa, *Philosophical Essays*
Elio Petri, *Writings on Cinema & Life*
Friedrich Nietzsche, *The Greek Music Drama*
Richard Foreman, *Plays with Films*
Louis-Auguste Blanqui, *Eternity by the Stars*
Miklós Szentkuthy, *Towards the One & Only Metaphor*
Josef Winkler, *When the Time Comes*
William Wordsworth, *Fragments*
Josef Winkler, *Natura Morta*
Fernando Pessoa, *The Transformation Book*
Emilio Villa, *The Selected Poetry of Emilio Villa*
Robert Kelly, *A Voice Full of Cities*
Pier Paolo Pasolini, *The Divine Mimesis*
Miklós Szentkuthy, *Prae, Vol. 1*
Federico Fellini, *Making a Film*
Robert Musil, *Thought Flights*
Sándor Tar, *Our Street*
Lorand Gaspar, *Earth Absolute*
Josef Winkler, *The Graveyard of Bitter Oranges*
Ferit Edgü, *Noone*
Jean-Jacques Rousseau, *Narcissus*
Ahmad Shamlu, *Born Upon the Dark Spear*
Jean-Luc Godard, *Phrases*
Otto Dix, *Letters, Vol. 1*
Maura Del Serra, *Ladder of Oaths*
Pierre Senges, *The Major Refutation*
Charles Baudelaire, *My Heart Laid Bare & Other Texts*
Joseph Kessel, *Army of Shadows*
Rainer J. Hanshe & Federico Gori, *Shattering the Muses*
Gérard Depardieu, *Innocent*
Claude Mouchard, *Entangled, Papers!, Notes*
Miklós Szentkuthy, *St. Orpheus Breviary, vol. II: Black Renaissance*
Adonis, *Conversations in the Pyrenees*

SOME FORTHCOMING TITLES

Iceberg Slim, *Night Train to Sugar Hill*
Rédoine Faid, *Bank Robber*

THE FUTURE OF KULCHUR
A PATRONAGE PROJECT

LEND CONTRA MUNDUM PRESS (CMP) YOUR SUPPORT

With bookstores and presses around the world struggling to survive, and many actually closing, we are forming this patronage project as a means for establishing a continuous & stable foundation to safeguard our longevity. Through this patronage project we would be able to remain free of having to rely upon government support &/or other official funding bodies, not to speak of their timelines & impositions. It would also free CMP from suffering the vagaries of the publishing industry, as well as the risk of submitting to commercial pressures in order to persist, thereby potentially compromising the integrity of our catalog.

CAN YOU SACRIFICE $10 A WEEK FOR KULCHUR?

For the equivalent of merely 2–3 coffees a week, you can help sustain CMP and contribute to the future of kulchur. To participate in our patronage program we are asking individuals to donate $500 per year, which amounts to $42/month, or $10/week. Larger donations are of course welcome and beneficial. All donations are tax-deductible through our fiscal sponsor Fractured Atlas. If preferred, donations can be made in two installments. We are seeking a minimum of 300 patrons per year and would like for them to commit to giving the above amount for a period of three years.

WHAT WE OFFER

Part tax-deductible donation, part exchange, for your contribution you will receive every CMP book published during the patronage period as well as 20 books from our back catalog. When possible, signed or limited editions of books will be offered as well.

WHAT WILL CMP DO WITH YOUR CONTRIBUTIONS?

Your contribution will help with basic general operating expenses, yearly production expenses (book printing, warehouse & catalog fees, etc.), advertising & outreach, and editorial, proofreading, translation, typography, design and copyright fees. Funds may also be used for participating in book fairs and staging events. Additionally, we hope to rebuild the *Hyperion* section of the website in order to modernize it.

From Pericles to Mæcenas & the Renaissance patrons, it is the magnanimity of such individuals that have helped the arts to flourish. Be a part of helping your kulchur flourish; be a part of history.

HOW

To lend your support & become a patron, please visit the subscription page of our website: contramundum.net/subscription

For any questions, write us at: info@contramundum.net

www.ingramcontent.com/pod-product-compliance
Lightning Source LLC
Chambersburg PA
CBHW031427160426
43195CB00010BB/638